# A WALK
# IN THE PARK

**Golfweek's**
America's
**BEST**
COURSES

## Bradley S. Klein
*and*
## Golfweek Magazine

FOREWORD BY TOM FAZIO

# A WALK IN THE PARK

## Golfweek's Guide to America's Best Classic and Modern Golf Courses

Publisher:
**Peter L. Bannon**

Developmental Editors:
**Doug Hoepker, Mark Zulauf**

Coordinating Editor:
**Scott Rauguth**

Photo Editor:
**Erin Linden-Levy**

Interior Design, Project Manager, Photo Imaging & Dust Jacket Design:
**Christine Mohrbacher**

Senior Managing Editors:
**Joseph J. Bannon Jr. and Susan M. Moyer**

Copy Editors:
**Holly Birch, Cindy McNew**

Major photographic contributions by John & Jeannine Henebry

**www.sportspublishingllc.com**
ISBN: 1-58261-605-1

**Mayacama Golf Club**
*Santa Rosa, California*

Classic Courses

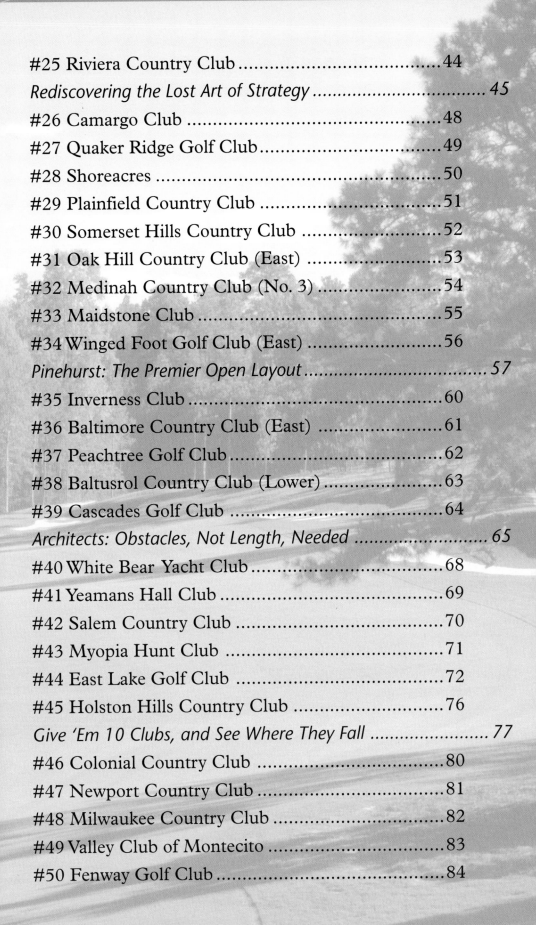

**Pinehurst Resort and Country Club (No**
*Pinehurst, North Carolina*

# Foreword

A unique part of *Golfweek's* course rankings is the magazine's educational workshop for its raters.

Twice, now, I've had the chance to speak at these meetings. I was happy to explain my work and to help the raters appreciate what modern architecture is all about. The first time, in 2001, we met at a course I did, Victoria National Golf Club in Newburgh, Indiana, No. 45 on the Modern List. A year later I spoke at a raters gathering in Pinehurst, N.C. On both occasions, I was impressed with the knowledge these raters had. They take their "job" seriously, travel a lot and form strong opinions. They also like to talk about their views and to question me about mine.

Although I don't always agree on "the rankings" and am sure most architects also have their own opinions, they do create a great forum for discussion and opinion. I have often said that there are literally hundreds of "Top 50" quality golf courses—it's mostly all just opinions.

Rating courses is not a science; it's a subjective experience. But ratings do have important consequences for the business of golf course architecture. Course owners, real estate developers, golf professionals and superintendents all keep an eye on the ratings and are influenced to some degree by what the lists identify as the superior courses. It's natural for people to feel good when others appreciate their work.

Golfers also benefit from these lists. It helps educate them as to what is considered good work. I sometimes think that golfers are like big-game hunters who take pride in bagging trophies. Playing a top-rated golf course is thus an achievement and sometimes an occasion for boasting.

Beyond the pleasure derived from playing such courses, it's important to explain the elements of what goes into course design. Criteria for good design include elements of routing, strategy, aesthetics and overall feel—what they call "the walk in the park." These are akin to the elements we as architects incorporate as we go about our design work. They're also the kinds of things that clients worry about when they are getting involved in a project.

In that sense, the course ratings are not just a beauty contest. They are also about improving the standards of golf course architecture.

I'm well into my fourth decade in the golf course design business. There's no question in my mind or the mind of anybody I know that golf courses are improving. Architects are smarter and better trained. Clients are more sophisticated in what they know and what they like. The techniques of course construction are more sophisticated. The folks building golf courses are more skilled than they've ever been. And the level of market competition for the eyes and dollars of the golfer is keener than ever, too. Clearly, this is one of those (many) cases where competition makes for a better product and a better experience.

I hope you enjoy reading about this in the pages that follow.

*Tom Fazio*

Tom Fazio
Hendersonville, N.C.
January 22, 2004

**Shadow Creek Golf Club**
*North Las Vegas, Nevada*

**Pine Valley Golf Club**
*Pine Valley, New Jersey*

# Welcome to the World of Golf Course Rankings

## By Bradley S. Klein

For many golfers, one of the most appealing aspects of the game is the nature of the playing fields. These are special places in terms of their shapes, their scale, their beauty and their settings.

Golfers of all skill levels jump at the chance to play a Pebble Beach or an Augusta National. Perhaps their grandeur is enhanced by the great tournaments that have been played there. What's certainly the case is that whatever the landform—be it desert, parkland or open meadow—the recognizably great golf courses convey a powerful aura that turns a round of golf into a spiritual journey. On such courses, the main reward comes not necessarily in playing well but in playing there at all.

As golfers, we are lucky to have such places to play. We're also blessed because the great golf courses are not just historic relics. While many of them date to the so-called Golden Age of golf course architecture in the period between World Wars I and II, a good number of them are of more recent vintage. In fact, they're still being created today. So instead of limiting ourselves to traditional courses, we've chosen in this book to include examples of the layouts that are going to be the trendsetters for the next century of golf as well. For every Pinehurst No. 2 to celebrate and honor, there's a Pacific Dunes or Whistling Straits that merits equal attention.

What makes a great golf course? Or a great golf hole? To some extent, we debate this every time we play golf or discuss a round afterward with our friends at the 19th hole. It's hard to improve on a statement made in 1920 by Alister MacKenzie in his book, *Golf Architecture*. The man who would go on to design Cypress Point Club and co-design Augusta National Golf Club was writing about individual holes, but the comment pertains just as readily to the overall course: "The ideal hole is surely one that affords the greatest pleasure to the greatest number, gives the fullest advantage for accurate play, stimulates players to improve their game, and never becomes monotonous."

The amazing thing about golf holes is how little they have in common. The rule book specifies only a single regulation—that the little cup we play for on each putting surface be four and a quarter inches in diameter. All else is up for grabs—terrain, elevation, soil, grasses and setting, as well as yardage and par.

When these elements are combined in an aesthetically pleasing way, we have the makings of greatness. Mere beauty isn't enough. The course must be intriguing, strategically challenging and perhaps even a bit whimsical to be recognized as great. Judging this is no easy matter. All golfers have their likes and dislikes when it comes to course design. The trick in golf, as in any endeavor, is to move beyond the realm of individual opinion and to arrive at a more systematic method of evaluation. The process might not be an exact science, but it certainly can be more than personal preference. Along the way, golfers might learn some things that will help them appreciate their own courses and to play better as well. What good is the business of rating unless it helps us enjoy the game more?

To that end, we at *Golfweek* have been identifying the country's finest golf courses since 1997. We call this compilation "America's Best." After treating our own subscribers to that list for the past seven years, we thought it was time to go to a wider golfing public. And so here's our updated version of the country's top 100 courses, broken down into the top 50 Classical and top 50 Modern layouts.

### Rating Classical and Modern

*Golfweek* has a team of 285 volunteer raters (representing 49 states) who perennially scour the countryside in search of superb and poor design. As we constantly hear, it's tough work, but someone has to do it. The 10 criteria we use, indicated below, include strategic considerations of shotmaking and design balance as well as the aesthetics of conditioning and setting. Our patented "walk in the park test" also is a crucial variable. It refers to the extent that the four or so hours spent at a course are worthwhile as an overall outdoor engagement.

What distinguishes our America's Best list from the course ratings done by other publications is a division of the golf course universe into two eras: Classical (up to 1959), and Modern (1960 and after). Why the split among the country's 17,000 courses? Roughly half of the existing stock predate 1960 and half postdate that year. More important are the era-specific differences in design, construction and grassing.

In earlier years, land for golf was so abundant that if a proposed site proved unsuitable, the architect would select an adjoining parcel. Older, traditional layouts were done by hand work and by animal-drawn labor. Little earth moving was possible, and the occasional blind shot was accepted as a sporting part of the game.

Features were built from existing grade, with putting surfaces "pushed up" from native soil. Routings—the sequence of holes—were intimate and easily walkable owing to close proximity of greens to tees. Real estate and cart paths were non-factors. No ground needed to be bypassed because no regulatory agencies controlled wetlands (they were called "swamps" back then), and developers were free to drain or fill them.

The design business changed rapidly around 1960. That's when national television, Arnold Palmer, bulldozers and suburban real estate all helped reshape the golf market. Robert Trent Jones Sr. led the way in creating new designs that favored power golf, the aerial game and the deployment of bunkering on the flanks of holes rather than diagonally or in the middle of fairways.

At the same time, the U.S. Golf Association Green Section introduced a more technically sophisticated method of layered greens construction that enabled a new generation of fine-bladed bentgrasses and Bermuda grasses to survive on greens at lower heights than had been imaginable two decades earlier. Soon, wetlands would be granted protected status, so the permitting process took considerably longer and land formerly usable for golf had to be circumvented. Architects found a solution to this routing problem in the form of the golf cart and tee-to-green paved paths. By the 1990s, anything was possible, a trend typified by the "heaven and earth" approach of Pete Dye, Tom Fazio and Jack Nicklaus. They were not averse to moving millions of cubic yards of earth in the course of creating layouts on land ill-suited to the purpose.

## Design Trends

Pine Valley Golf Club in Pine Valley, New Jersey, and Sand Hills Golf Club in Mullen, Nebraska, are ranked No. 1, respectively, on our Classical and Modern lists. Each has stood atop our rating list since we began publishing the rankings in 1997. Donald Ross (12 courses) is the leader of the Classical-era designers when it comes to ranked courses on the America's Best list. On the Modern side, the top designers are Pete Dye and Tom Fazio, each with nine original layouts ranked (Fazio also has two major Classical renovations to his credit). Interestingly, these designers typify the era in which they worked. Ross was a genius in using native contours to create holes that played from high point (tee) to high point (fairway landing area) to high point (putting surface and surrounds). Dye and Fazio, by contrast, are modern masters in creating something when the land doesn't provide it. A prime example of this approach can be seen at Shadow Creek in Las Vegas (No. 6 Modern), where Fazio created more than 100 feet of elevation change on what had been a dead flat site, then planted the barren ground with 21,000 trees to create 18 theatre-stage golf holes (complete with backdrop).

How good are the new designs? We just might be in a second Golden Age. After all, the 1990s produced exactly as many top-ranked courses on our list—25—as the 1920s. For all the development of fine new layouts in recent years, the 1920s remain the single most productive decade when it comes to defining an era of great golf course architecture.

Although fine design used to be an elite domain, it's now becoming more publicly accessible. The Classical list includes 46 private courses and only four public-access courses. Of these, three are resorts and only one is truly daily-fees: No. 21 Bethpage State Park's Black Course in Farmingdale, N.Y., a U.S. Open venue in 2002 (and 2009) at which state residents can play for as little as $31. The Modern list is considerably more publicly oriented, with 34 privates, 10 resorts and six daily-fees.

## Modern Diversity

The Modern era is by no means singular in style. Recent years have seen the rise of a more naturalistic model of architecture that evokes traditional design principles and allows the land to determine the routing and shape of holes. These courses are built with high-tech machinery and maintained with state-of-the-art, multi-row irrigation systems and small hydraulic mowing units. And yet they look decades old. The chief proponents of this lower-profile approach have been Bill Coore and Ben Crenshaw, with three courses rated—Sand Hills, Friar's Head (No. 11) and Cuscowilla on Lake Oconee (No. 13). Tom Doak, with two leading designs to his credit on the Modern list—Pacific Dunes (No. 2) and Lost Dunes (No. 41)—is another up-and-coming advocate of this school of thought.

Restoration and renovation also figure prominently, which comes as no surprise in a time when the golf course development market is shifting from building new courses to tinkering with established ones. Gil Hanse's restoration of A.W. Tillinghast's Fenway Golf Club (No. 50 Classical) has brought that previously unheralded layout into some pretty heady company. Two or three decades ago, the talk was all about "modernization," and in the process some quirky old features and a lot of 6,500-yard long classical courses were robbed of their character in the name of updating them. Today, heritage and tradition are valued, and restoration is in vogue. The shift in perspectives is partly due to the limelight accorded U.S. Open venues. The trend began in 1986 when the golf world saw how challenging Shinnecock Hills (No. 3 Classical) was for the world's finest golfer. Two years later at The Country Club (No. 23 Classical), architect Rees Jones' meticulous retrofitting of the original design by Howard C. Toomey and William S. Flynn was met

### America's Best by Access

|  | Private (p) | Resort (r) | Daily-Fee (d) |
|---|---|---|---|
| **Classical:** | 46 | 3 | 1 |
| **Modern:** | 34 | 10 | 6 |
| **Total** | 80 | 13 | 7 |

### America's Best By Decade (according to main year of its development):

- 1890-99: ▬ (3)
- 1900-09: ▬ (3)
- 1910-19: ▬▬▬▬▬ (11)
- 1920-29: ▬▬▬▬▬▬▬▬▬▬▬ (25)
- 1930-39: ▬▬▬ (7)
- 1940-49: ▌(1)
- 1950-59: (0)
- 1960-69: ▬▬▬ (7)
- 1970-79: ▌(1)
- 1980-89: ▬▬▬ (8)
- 1990-99: ▬▬▬▬▬▬▬▬▬▬▬ (25)
- 2000-present: ▬▬ (9)

### America's Best by Architect (architects with three or more courses in rankings)

|  | Classic | Modern | Total |
|---|---|---|---|
| Donald J. Ross | 12 | – | 12 |
| Tom Fazio | 2 | 9 | 11 |
| A.W. Tillinghast | 10 | – | 10 |
| Pete Dye | – | 9 | 9 |
| Alister MacKenzie | 4 | – | 4 |
| Jack Nicklaus | – | 3 | 3 |
| Seth Raynor | 5 | – | 5 |
| Robert Trent Jones Sr. | 3 | 3 | 6 |
| Rees Jones | 1 | 3 | 4 |
| Bill Coore | – | 3 | 3 |
| Ben Crenshaw | – | 3 | 3 |
| William S. Flynn | 3 | – | 3 |
| Jay Morrish | – | 3 | 3 |
| Tom Weiskopf | – | 3 | 3 |

with universal acclaim. Since then, many courses on our Classical list have improved their playing character by identifying and deepening their traditional features.

Similarly, some Modern courses have enjoyed the fruits of renovations by their original architects. At the Ocean Course at Kiawah Island (No. 16), Dye recently improved visibility of the landing areas and provided a stronger finishing hole. At Atlantic Golf Club (No. 49), Rees Jones and superintendent Bob Ranum squared off the tees and took out protective containment mounding for a sharper, more traditional fallaway look around the greens.

This wasn't tinkering. This was systematic planning with the intent of bringing out the playing character and offering more interesting shotmaking options. Beauty, aesthetics and setting are fine, but they are not enough to ensure a great golf course. Without great options and alternative paths to play the holes, a course can't be considered truly outstanding.

The business of ratings might not be a science. But it's certainly more than mere personal taste. You might not agree with our choices—or our reasoning. But our hope is that you'll at least learn something from this evaluation that will be of use to you the next time you play—and that you'll appreciate your own golf course more as a result.

## Criteria of Evaluation for America's Best Course Ratings

### 1. Ease and intimacy of routing

The extent to which the sequence of holes follows natural contours and unfolds in an unforced manner.

### 2a. Integrity of original design (Classical)

The extent to which subsequent changes are compatible with the original design and enhance the course rather than undermine or weaken it.

### 2b. Quality of feature shaping (Modern)

The extent to which the land's features have been enhanced though earth moving and shaping to form a landscape that suits the game and has aesthetic/thematic coherence.

### 3. Natural setting and overall land plan

Quality and aesthetic relationship of golf course, clubhouse, cart paths and other facility features to surrounding structures and native scenery.

### 4. Interest of greens and surrounding contours

Shotmaking demands on and around the putting surfaces.

### 5. Variety and memorability of par 3s

Different clubs hit; different terrain; different looks.

### 6. Variety and memorability of par 4s

The extent to which the angles of play, varied terrain and left-to-right/right-to-left shots create interesting and varied playing options.

### 7. Variety and memorability of par 5s

The extent to which holes offer a variety of options from the tee and on the second shot as well as risk/reward possibilities.

### 8. Basic quality of conditioning

Variety of playing textures; extent of turf coverage; consistency and quality of bunker sand; delineation of tees/fairways/roughs/collars and chipping areas (beyond day-to-day changes because of weather, aerification, overseeding or repairs).

### 9. Landscape and tree management

The extent to which trees and any floral features complement or enhance rather than impose and intrude upon the ground features and the playing options of the course.

### 10. "Walk in the park" test

The degree to which the course is ultimately worth spending a half-day on as a compelling outdoor experience.

# Classic Courses

**The Olympic Club**
*San Francisco, California*

*Classic course profile*

**Architects:** George Crump & H. S. Colt, 1914-1919     **Superintendent:** Richard E. Christian Jr.

# Pine Valley Golf Club

## Pine Valley, New Jersey

Golfers like to talk about the pain this course inflicts, but to the person who appreciates excellent design, precise shotmaking and unparalleled variety, Pine Valley is also about pleasure. It's the pleasure of purity and a club that is all golf. It's the pleasure of those sandy waste areas and the treacherous bunkering. It's about sleeping in the dormitory and feasting on the snapper soup. It's watching a videotape of the sport's version of *The Shining*—the "Shell's Wonderful World of Golf" match in which Gene Littler cards a quadruple-bogey 7 on the 232-yard fifth hole, sending viewers scurrying for another round (of drinks, that is). But most importantly, it is about the most complete 18 holes in the land.

There is, for example, the opener, a seemingly benign par 4 that is the source of more 6s than the devil himself. And the par-5 seventh has the famed "Hell's Half Acre," a scrubby expanse that must be carried with your second shot if there is to be any hope of par. Then there's No. 8, where a good drive leaves most golfers with only a wedge to either of the alternate greens. But both are so small in size that only a perfect shot ever seems to hold.

Things only get better on the back, starting with the par-3 10th and its renowned front bunker, said to have been named for "Satan's least attractive body part." The 13th is regarded by many as one of the best par 4s in golf; there is something special here about hitting a drive to the top of the hill, then drawing a long, downhill iron to a green that looks big enough to accommodate a helicopter landing. Then you finish with three brilliant par 4s, especially No. 18, which requires a strong drive and long iron to a roomy green, bringing the round to a thrilling close.

Is there pain at Pine Valley? Yes indeed. But it always offers much more pleasure.

—*John Steinbreder*

| Par | 70 |
|---|---|
| Yards | 6,699 |
| Slope | 153 |
| Rating | 74.1 |

**Golfweek Rating**
**9.65**

# Cypress Point Club

## Monterey, California

Around at this small, ultra-private retreat begins with only subtle hints of great things to come: a tee shot over a hedge and a stretch of the famed 17 Mile Drive to an unseen fairway, a spacious green set some 400 yards away on the crest of a dune, a sliver of the Pacific Ocean visible far off and to the left and a windswept wisp of fog drifting from the shore. Listen quietly, and you can hear the sounds of waves breaking and sea lions barking. Once you have hit your drive, you are off on one of the finest walks in golf.

The course at Cypress Point leads you quickly from that first dune up into a pine forest. Then it takes you back onto the dunes and to the craggy ocean shore. The acclaimed Alister MacKenzie worked wonders with his design, mainly because he let Mother Nature, not conventional wisdom, determine the length and layout of the holes. Distances from the blue and white tees hardly seem intimidating, and you have consecutive par 5s (Nos. 5 and 6), par 3s (Nos. 15 and 16) and short par 4s (Nos. 8 and 9).

A setup like that does not make much sense—or much of an impression—on paper, but it works magnificently in practice. The round builds to a rousing crescendo on Nos. 15, 16 and 17, all of which run along the Pacific and are so visually and architecturally breathtaking that they have been known to cause hyperventilation in first-time players.

Cypress Point often has that same effect on regulars, some of whom have been heard to remark that in their views, heaven would be only a lateral move from this hallowed track.

—*John Steinbreder*

| | |
|---|---|
| **Par** | 72 |
| **Yards** | 6,524 |
| **Slope** | 136 |
| **Rating** | 72.4 |

**Golfweek Rating**
9.63

**Architects:** Howard C. Toomey & William S. Flynn, 1931    **Superintendent:** Mark Michaud

# Shinnecock Hills Golf Club

## Southampton, New York

Shinnecock Hills is a showcase of natural-looking design, yet there is nothing soft about it. During U.S. Opens there in 1986 (won by Raymond Floyd) and 1995 (Corey Pavin), it demonstrated that for all its elegance and apparent simplicity, it also could be among the world's most fearsome courses as a championship venue.

The club was incarnated in 1891 for that new class of high society that had begun summering nearby in the town of Southampton, 100 miles east of Central Park, on a sandy strip of Long Island's south fork. Overlooking the windswept site is a distinctive white clapboard clubhouse designed by famed architect Stanford White in the regional "East End" style. The club, one of five founding members of the USGA in 1894, also made history in the mid-1890s when it built the country's first "ladies' course."

The present layout has been there, virtually unchanged, since 1931, when it was designed and built by William Flynn and Howard Toomey. The course fills 256 acres, yet there are no long walks from tee to green. The putting surfaces, only 5,500 square feet, are open up front and allow for run-up shots.

Among the truly ingenious aspects of Shinnecock's design is the staggered positioning of fairway bunkers. At two uphill par 4s, the 12th (477 yards) and the 14th (444 yards), a trio of bunkers flanking each fairway sets up optional avenues off the tee.

Several new back tees will be added for the 2004 U.S. Open—about 100 yards total. That's a minor concession to the modern game. With all of its ground-game character, Shinnecock Hills doesn't need to pile on distance to challenge modern golfers.

—*Bradley S. Klein*

| | |
|---|---|
| **Par** | 70 |
| **Yards** | 6,944 |
| **Slope** | 144 |
| **Rating** | 74.6 |

**Golfweek Rating**
9.19

# Augusta National Golf Club

## Augusta, Georgia

There probably is no more exhilarating sensation in golf than walking to the first tee at Augusta National and getting ready to hit your drive. It is not the design of the hole that does it, of course, but the anticipation of an entire round at the club that hosts the Masters, sets the gold standard for conditioning and has arguably the richest history of any track in America. It's the brilliant white of the sand in the gaping fairway bunker, the luscious green of the grass, the subtle brown of the pine needles raked in perfect circles at the base of the trees and the knowledge that many of golf's greatest players have walked that very ground. It's like writing at Hemingway's desk or painting at Brueghel's easel.

But Augusta is more than great atmosphere. It also is a marvelous layout with terrific variety and devilish design. If you know how to work the ball, especially right to left, and are confident with your putter, you can score well, provided you keep your heart rate at reasonable levels. And that is very hard to do, especially as you make your way around Amen Corner. Perhaps the three best shots of the day come beginning with the approach to the par-4 11th (don't come over the top and pull-hook an iron into the drink) and continuing with the tee shot on the par-3 12th (no green has ever felt narrower) and the drive on the par-5 13th, where you stand back among the azaleas and draw a ball nearly around the corner.

Augusta National is built on the site of an old nursery and is replete with gorgeous stands of trees and beautiful beds of plants and flowers. It is also cathedral-quiet. That seems appropriate, for playing the track that winds through and over these grounds is very much a religious experience.

*—John Steinbreder*

| | |
|---|---|
| **Par** | 72 |
| **Yards** | 7,290 |
| **Slope** | N/A |
| **Rating** | N/A |

**Golfweek Rating**
**9.18**

**Architects:** Jack Neville & Douglas Grant, 1919    **Superintendent:** Tom Huesgen

# Pebble Beach Golf Links

## Pebble Beach, California

*Classic course profile*

Jack Nicklaus says it is his favorite course. So do Tom Watson and Johnny Miller. If you polled the thousands of golfers who play Pebble Beach Golf Links each year, you would find that most of them feel the same.

It can take a while for those feelings to take hold during a round because the first three holes are unspectacular at best. But then the course starts to work its way south along the rocky Pacific Ocean shore and its magic suddenly appears.

It's hard deciding what the best parts of that stretch are. Maybe it is walking up the hill on the par-5 sixth and getting your first look at that green and the water beyond. Or perhaps, it's the testy wedge you have to float downhill to the tiny green of the par-3 seventh. Then there's the second shot on No. 8, over that treacherous chasm to the well-bunkered green. Listen carefully, and you can hear the sea lions bark as you try to settle on your distance.

Fortunately, the pleasure of Pebble Beach does not end there. For one thing, the Pacific stays more or less in view even as the course takes you back to the north and a bit inland. The 12th is a deceptively tough par 3 that requires a crisp long iron to a small green guarded by four bunkers. The par-5 14th is next to impossible to reach in less than three shots and has what may well be the most difficult green on the course.

At the 17th, it is hard not to gawk at the Pacific beyond that hourglass-shaped green and think about Tom Watson's famous wedge shot that secured his U.S. Open victory in 1982. The 18th is all about water, waves and wind. All that is missing for those playing this resort course are the bleachers and television towers set up for the annual AT&T Pebble Beach National Pro-Am tournament and the crowds cheering each shot.

*—John Steinbreder*

| | |
|---|---|
| **Par** | 72 |
| **Yards** | 6,828 |
| **Slope** | 144 |
| **Rating** | 74.3 |

***Golfweek* Rating**
**9.11**

# Oakmont Country Club

## Oakmont, Pennsylvania

That Oakmont has been designated a National Historic Landmark is all you need to know. As the site of 17 national championships (including the 2003 U.S. Amateur and the 2007 U.S. Open), it is one of the country's storied golf grounds. It was at Oakmont that Bobby Jones won the 1925 U.S. Amateur; Ben Hogan won the 1953 U.S. Open; Jack Nicklaus beat Arnold Palmer in an 18-hole playoff for the 1962 Open title; and Johnny Miller produced his magical 63 to win the 1973 Open.

Oakmont is renown for its speed-of-light greens and "church pew" bunkering. However, the course underwent a dramatic facelift in 2001, when thousands of trees were removed and 90 yards added to its championship length. The results were extraordinary, as Oakmont regained the wide-open links characteristics originally envisioned by architect Henry Fownes when he fashioned this gem on a plateau overlooking the Allegheny River.

Matching par at Oakmont is a daunting task, thanks to revisions made post-1911 by William Fownes, son of Henry and winner of the 1910 U.S. Amateur. His goal was to make it the world's most difficult test of golf. This was consistent with his observation that "A shot poorly played should be a shot irrevocably lost."

A century after its founding, Oakmont remains a club for serious golfers who understand and appreciate its legacy.

—*Dave Seanor*

| | |
|---|---|
| **Par** | 71 |
| **Yards** | 7,018 |
| **Slope** | 144 |
| **Rating** | 76.2 |

**Golfweek Rating**
9.00

**Classic** *course profile*

**Architect:** Hugh Wilson, 1912    **Superintendent:** Matthew G. Shaffer

# Merion Golf Club (East)

## Ardmore, Pennsylvania

| Par | 70 |
|---|---|
| Yards | 6,482 |
| Slope | 142 |
| Rating | 73.6 |

**Golfweek Rating**

**8.95**

Too bad there won't be another U.S. Open at Merion.

The four there, in 1934, 1950, 1971 and 1981, all have been closely contested, which is what happens when you put the world's finest players on a shotmaker's course and ask them to play precise position golf. The pros today drive the ball so far they'd all be laying up off the tee and still be hitting flip wedges into most of the par 4s. But as everyday amateur players find out when they get to this fabled layout on Philadelphia's east side, yardage has nothing to do with the challenges posed by the firm, rolling fairways and tightly bunkered greens.

The sense of playing at special place starts on the first hole, a perfect dogleg right of 362 yards. Folks lunching on the veranda have put down their iced drinks momentarily lest the tinkling disturb nearby players on the tee.

As with every great golf course, there are some routing anomalies at Merion that do not conform to any of the so-called "rules" that architects are supposed to follow.

The only par 5s on the course are at the second and fourth holes. There also is an amazingly delicate stretch, Nos. 7-13, where the yardages read like nothing else in U.S. tournament golf: 350-360-193-310-369-371-127. The course ends with a trio of long, demanding holes that incorporate abandoned quarry ground. The last of them, the 463-yard 18th, was the scene of one of the most famous photographs in golf—Ben Hogan's finish to the 1-iron he hit to the 72nd green at the 1950 U.S. Open.

—*Bradley S. Klein*

# Nirvana Country Club by Design

## *No Pool, No Cell Phones, Just Golf*

### By John Steinbreder

The question is one my friends and I often ponder after a round, and it really is quite simple: What makes a golf club great?

The obvious first answer is that a great club must have a great course. But there are many other factors involved.

A great golf club has small scorecards, primarily white, about the size of playing cards when folded, and not illustrated with photographs. Like Augusta National's. Pencils with erasers are a nice touch, too.

A great golf club also has a small but well-appointed pro shop, and the first tee is just a short walk away, which is what you'll find at Cypress Point and Riviera. It is a place that has a fabulous porch (Shinnecock) and at least one signature drink (Southsides, again at Shinnecock) or dish (snapper soup at Pine Valley, or perhaps freshly cooked lobster at the National Golf Links). But the food never comes close to overshadowing the course. You talk about the quality of the layout when you leave, not the lunchtime buffet.

A great golf club has a strong caddie program, a small fleet of golf carts that are available only to those who have legitimate medical excuses, and a head professional who got his start in the caddie shack or the bag room. It is the sort of spot where touring pros and top amateurs play on their days off.

A great golf club does not have to institute a "No Cell Phone" policy because the membership is so old that no one has a cell phone or knows how to operate one, and even if they did, it would never occur to them to bring one on the course. It also is where you will find an honor system at the practice range and at the halfway house. Members at clubs like that have no interest in cheating each other out of a few bucks.

Speaking of halfway houses, a great golf club has only the most austere setup for those mid-round breaks. It does not have monstrous walk-in refrigerators or ultramodern hot dog grills, but rather the simplest selection of drinks and snacks, and maybe even a day-old sandwich or two. After all, we are only talking about a four-hour round here, not a five-day desert march, and it seems ridiculous for anyone to need—or want—much more.

A great golf club still has a men's grill room, no matter how politically incorrect that may be, and is the sort of place that might require a jacket in the bar but has no dress code on the course (such as Garden City, where members can play in the nude for all they care). All the flags on the greens are the same color (yes, you have to figure out where the pin is by yourself), and there are no GPS systems or yardage markers. It also is a spot that is so old and traditional that it can no longer host a U.S. Open, either because it lacks parking (Merion), length (Merion, again) or the inclination to be overrun by hordes of golf fans—and the U.S. Golf Association—just for a little extra money and recognition.

A great golf club has only a short walk between all the greens and tees (Cypress Point, again) and a course designed by an architect who long ago went on to his great reward (such as Macdonald, Raynor, MacKenzie, Ross or Tillinghast). And at some point during your round you play one of the great holes from the British Isles, whether it's a Redan, Road Hole, Postage Stamp or Biarritz.

Great golf clubs do not have swimming pools. Or if they do, they are cracked, empty and more or less abandoned like the one at Chicago Golf, or completely unused, as is the case at Seminole. They also have very small or inactive memberships, so the courses are almost always empty and the pace of play delightfully quick. I have played 36 holes at Chicago Golf with two other fellows in just over six hours. And the one time I teed it up at San Francisco Golf Club, I saw only one other group on the course. On a Saturday afternoon, no less, and it was a fivesome that finished in about four hours.

A great golf club understands how special an experience it offers first-timers and makes a point of treating its guests as well as its members. That's one of the many things that makes Augusta and Pine Valley so good.

And greatness must be bestowed on any club that is able to maintain the same feel and character over the years. Like this venerable spot I know in New England that not too long ago looked into renovating its clubhouse.

When the estimated price soared too high for those old-line Yankees, they started scrounging for ways to cut back. One suggestion: Instead of replacing the floorboards of the expansive porch, which had been pocked with spike marks, they would simply flip over the wood and use the other side. It sounded good to one and all, but when workers turned over the first boards, they found that previous club leaders had had the same idea some decades before.

As for the name of that wonderful place, it is something readers are going to have to do without, because the club boasts one other element that makes it—and those like it—great. And that is having utter disdain—or ambivalence—when it comes to publicity.

Especially when it means being mentioned in a column like this.

# "A great golf course does not have to institute a 'No Cell Phone' policy because the membership is so old that no one has a cell phone..."

**Architect:** Charles Blair Macdonald, 1911    **Superintendent:** William B. Salinetti III, CGCS

# National Golf Links of America

## Southampton, New York

A documentary film about American course design would start with the National Golf Links of America on the far southern shore of eastern Long Island. There, an egomaniacal golf patriarch by the name of Charles Blair Macdonald translated the best holes and features of British linksland golf onto an American landscape.

There on a sandy, windswept setting between Shinnecock Hills Golf Club and Peconic Bay, "C. B." and his site engineer, a newcomer to course design named Seth Raynor, brought to life a Hall of Fame of holes: the short par-4 concept of Sahara; the severe uphill second-shot challenge of Alps; the diagonal greenside hazard and fallaway putting surface of the Redan par 3. They didn't copy the Road Hole bunker or the short par-3 Eden from St. Andrews, but those features work. They also were smart enough to create wide corridors of play off the tee to create multiple routes and room for the wind to play havoc with the ball.

Years of overgrowth had closed down some original lines of play, but longtime National Golf Links superintendent Karl Olson, CGCS, made it his personal quest during his stint at the club (1986-2002) to reclaim those areas and restore the golf course's playing character. Those now in charge of National Golf Links have an immense responsibility—to preserve the game's living museum. If a certain class of modern country club golfer doesn't get the point of the links-style game played here, they are best accommodated elsewhere. National Golf Links is for tweedy old purists and students of the classical game.

*—Bradley S. Klein*

| | |
|---|---|
| **Par** | 73 |
| **Yards** | 6,779 |
| **Slope** | 141 |
| **Rating** | 74.3 |

**Golfweek Rating**
8.84

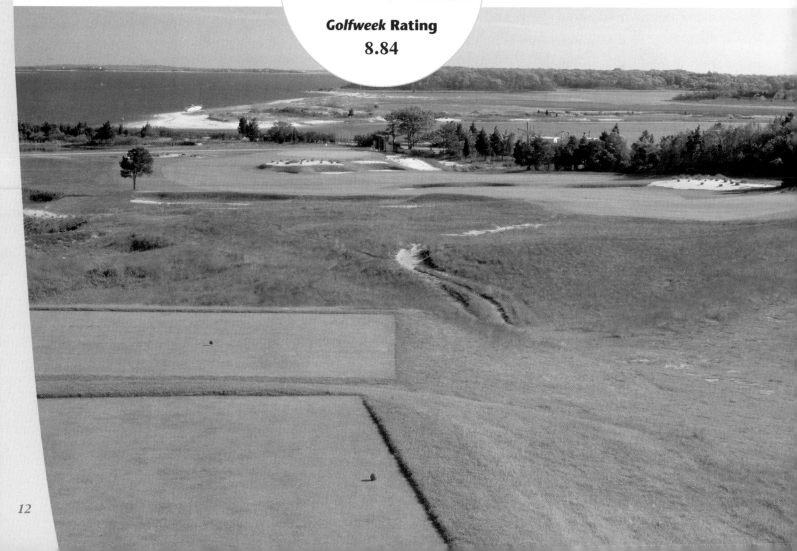

**Architects:** Alister MacKenzie & Perry Maxwell, 1931   **Superintendent:** Michael Morris, CGCS

# Crystal Downs Country Club

## Frankfort, Michigan

| Par | 70 |
|---|---|
| Yards | 6,518 |
| Slope | 138 |
| Rating | 73.6 |

*Golfweek* **Rating**
**8.82**

Situated on a bluff overlooking Lake Michigan, far from any metropolitan areas, Crystal Downs is one of the lesser-known masterpieces designed by Dr. Alister MacKenzie. The project was sandwiched between his work on Cypress Point and Augusta National.

Wind is always a factor at "The Downs." A deft short game is required, for its green contours are among the most severe and challenging anywhere. The horseshoe green at No. 7 is the epitome of quirky. The native Northern Michigan rough is thick and punishing.

Best thing about Crystal Downs is the way it challenges course management skills. It may be only 6,518 yards and par 70, but it's hardly benign. Four par 4s under 360 yards can yield ecstasy or disaster. Contemporary architect and course critic Tom Doak said it best: "Simply put, if you haven't seen Crystal Downs, your education in golf architecture is incomplete."

—**Dave Seanor**

**Architect:** Donald J. Ross, 1903-1946     **Superintendent:** Paul Jett, CGCS

# Pinehurst Resort and Country Club (No. 2)

## Pinehurst, North Carolina

### Ross' Masterpiece Challenges All

*By Bradley S. Klein*

Take wide-open fairways, remove water and out-of-bounds as elements to contend with, then give mowed-down areas around the putting surfaces for perfect lies on every recovery shot. Then stand back and take perverse pleasure as generation after generation of golfers—of every skill level—come to grief on simple-looking holes.

Ah, but those greens. Turtle-backed, slick and rolling off every-which-direction into bunkers, low-lying collection areas or dead flat spots. No wonder only one player could break par there in the 1999 U.S. Open—and winner Payne Stewart did so by only one stroke.

The Pinehurst No. 2 course, the personal handiwork of designer Donald J. Ross (1872-1948), continually poses distinctive challenges to golfers who think they can have their way here. In fact, the better the golfer, the harder this course plays. Higher handicappers usually love the place because they can get around with one golf ball per round and can play the ball safely down the middle. But the same conditions that make this course relatively benign for high handicappers play havoc on the scores of good golfers, who continually face shots to marginal pins that allow no room for error.

A good rule of thumb here is to forget about hole placements and play instead for the front third of every green. Short-game options run the gamut from the lob wedge to middle irons and even fairway woods or putters. Ross designed the course to play hard and firm, and the course setup, which included no rough around any of the greens, enabled the architect's intentions to come through. A golf course tweaked by its designer for decades after its inception and that only got its grass greens in 1935 continues to shows its relevance today.

| Par | 72 |
|---|---|
| Yards | 7,210 |
| Slope | 135 |
| Rating | 75.3 |

**Golfweek Rating**
8.63

As a resort course with a private membership component, No. 2 gets a lot of play. The Pinehurst Resort's other seven courses are each intriguing in their own right, but guests should make sure they have access to No. 2 for at least one round. First time on the layout, throw away your ego and play from one set of tees forward of what you think you can handle, whether at yardages of 6,741 (blue), 6,309 (white), 5,836 (green) or 5,035 (red). If you hit anything longer than mid-irons into these greens you have no chance of holding them, so choose your tees accordingly.

## America's Best: Rater's Notebook

### 1. Ease and intimacy of routing: 10

A nice easy walk out and back, with an opening hole that feels part of the town—complete with a white church spire in view. You literally roll off/roll on from one green to the next tee.

### 2. Integrity of original design: 10

For a course that evolved in phases—the newest holes (Nos. 4 and 5) were added in 1935—there's been plenty of time for everything to settle in uniformly.

### 3. Natural setting and overall land plan: 9

Amazing how five courses all radiate out from one central clubhouse, with the practice greens and learning facility ("Maniac Hill") centrally positioned to all of them. The modicum of housing on the front nine of No. 2 is set back and seems to enhance rather than detract. The only sore point is a rigid, linear clubhouse whose roofline counteracts the effect of the 18th hole.

### 4. Interest of greens and surrounding contours: 9

Contours are bold beyond belief—a bit severe on the "yikes meter" for modern play when the speeds are up. The bentgrass greens are so firm and tightly knit that only a perfectly spun shot will hold. Only about half of each green (average size: 6,000 square feet) is level enough to accommodate a hole placement, meaning that the effective target area of each green is really closer to 3,000 square feet. Maddening, but loads of fun—unless you're trying to turn in a score. There's no such thing as a good approach shot until you see where—and whether—it comes to rest.

### 5. Variety and memorability of par 3s: 6

If you've selected the proper set of markers from the outset, you should be hitting a good range of mid-irons into these greens. The propped-up ninth green is visually striking because it looks like there's no place to land the ball. The sixth and 15th are not impressive-looking but are demanding to play because the greens seem to repel the ball.

### 6. Variety and memorability of par 4s: 8

Generous fairways, with very few bunkers influencing tee shots. This is a second-shot golf course all the way. The par-4 holes tend to grind away at you, and while the longest of them (the fifth) and the shortest (the uphill 13th) are memorable, the rest mainly have the effect of wearing you down.

### 7. Variety and memorability of par 5s: 7

All of the strategy here is on the second shots, a matter dictated as much by hole placement and angle of approach as by bunkers in the secondary landing areas short of the greens.

### 8. Basic quality of conditioning: 7

Kept firm and fast, with lots of labor-intensive mowing needed for chipping areas around putting surfaces. Plays best in summer when dry; winter overseed tends to play just a bit slower and heavier than is ideal.

### 9. Landscape and tree management: 8

Steady tree work and the occasional winter storm have done a good job of keeping canopies out of play. They've avoided cluttering the place with flowerbeds. Hitting out of the pine straw areas makes recovery a guessing game, which is precisely what should happen when you're in marginal areas.

### 10. "Walk in the park" test: 9

Easy to walk, though management treats it otherwise. If you don't take a caddie, you're required to ride a cart and are confined to distant paths. What an awful way to play No.2. By the way, the caddies are so wise about the lay of the land here that they can read any putt on the course—from the clubhouse.

*Overall vote by Golfweek course raters: 8.63*

| Hole | 1 | 2 | 3 | 4 | 5 | 6 | 7 | 8 | 9 | Out | Card of the Course |
|---|---|---|---|---|---|---|---|---|---|---|---|
| Yardage | 403 | 449 | 340 | 550 | 483 | 224 | 404 | 487 | 190 | 3,530 | |
| Par | 4 | 4 | 4 | 5 | 4 | 3 | 4 | 5 | 3 | 36 | |
| Hole | 10 | 11 | 12 | 13 | 14 | 15 | 16 | 17 | 18 | In | Total |
| Yardage | 611 | 452 | 446 | 381 | 437 | 205 | 516 | 187 | 445 | 3,680 | 7,210 |
| Par | 5 | 4 | 4 | 4 | 4 | 3 | 5 | 3 | 4 | 36 | 72 |

Classic *course profile*

**Architect:** Seth Raynor, 1926 **Superintendent:** Donald Beck

# Fishers Island Golf Club

## Fishers Island, New York

Samuel Coleridge could have been describing Fishers Island when he wrote "Rime of the Ancient Mariner" and those opening words, "Water, water everywhere..." After all, the glorious Seth Raynor layout on the tiny cay in Long Island Sound is accessible only by boat and has water views on every hole.

True to form, Raynor created stunning versions of the great holes of the Old World, beginning in this case with a 172-yard Redan on No. 2, which has a plateau green that is angled at 45 degrees from the tee and tilted dramatically from the left front to the rear. That's followed by the Punch Bowl fourth (one of only two holes at Fishers without bunkers) and the Biarritz fifth, a long par 3 based largely on a hole designed by Willie Dunn in Biarritz, France, in the late 1880s. It has a deep swale in front of the green, two bunkers on each side, a bay to the right and some of the best vistas on the course. There also is a Double Plateau (No. 9) as well as an Eden (11th) and Cape (14th).

Half the fun at Fishers Island can be getting there. Private boats can pull into the club pier by the 17th green, and golfers can load their sticks onto carts left by the pro shop and drive up to the shingled clubhouse at the top of the hill. You can warm up by hitting shag balls into Barley Field Cove (there is no range) or stroking a few putts on the practice green. Then it's off for a round on as good a links as you will find in this country—especially when the wind blows hard off the Sound and the balls bounce firmly on the dry summer ground.

*—John Steinbreder*

| | |
|---|---|
| **Par** | 72 |
| **Yards** | 6,544 |
| **Slope** | 136 |
| **Rating** | 72.6 |

***Golfweek* Rating**
**8.61**

**Architect:** A. W. Tillinghast, 1922    **Superintendent:** Bob Klinestekker

# San Francisco Golf Club

## San Francisco, California

Founded by four Scotsman from Fife and Angus in 1895, San Francisco Golf Club is located in the extreme southwest corner of town, just on the near side of Lake Merced. No one is sure exactly who designed the initial 18-hole track that stood at that location, but it was the site of some terrific golf. Harry Vardon and Ted Ray played an exhibition there, and Walter Hagen won the Panama Pacific International Open on the layout, shooting a remarkable 29 on his final nine.

It wasn't until A. W. Tillinghast came to town in 1921 and began revamping the entire layout, however, that San Francisco also became known for its excellent design. Working on what essentially was a treeless, sandy expanse that featured rolling dunes and occasional views of the Pacific Ocean, he created a seaside-style links course that ranks among his best efforts. Members of the elite club, which boasts a pleasingly discreet pro shop and low-key, no-nonsense air, describe the track as "a mysterious joy" and "beautifully treacherous."

There are no water hazards, fairways are wide, and the greens are ample and incomparably conditioned. Par remains elusive to even the lowest handicappers. Yet players always leave the course with a sense of calm and satisfaction, so pristine and pure is the experience of walking these 18 holes. The apparent ease and naturalness of the grounds requires constant attention—most recently through a massive restoration effort in which trees were felled and putting surfaces expanded to recapture their original boldness.

The hole that stands out most of all is No. 7, a testy, downhill play that Tillinghast once described as the best par 3 he ever built. It also is noteworthy because it was the site of the last legal duel in the United States, the place where U.S. Senator David Broderick and California Supreme Court Justice David Terry settled a dispute over slavery in 1859. Broderick reportedly got the yips when it came time to draw his pistol. Terry drilled him with a shot, and the senator died a few days later.

Today, that hole—and the course—treats golfers with much greater hospitality.

—*John Steinbreder*

| | |
|---|---|
| **Par** | 71 |
| **Yards** | 6,754 |
| **Slope** | 134 |
| **Rating** | 73.0 |

**Golfweek Rating**

8.55

**Architects:** Perry Maxwell, 1937 • Press Maxwell, 1957    **Superintendent:** Philip D. George, CGCS

# Prairie Dunes Country Club

## Hutchinson, Kansas

### Maxwell's Natural Prairie Dunes a Piece of Plains Paradise

*By Bradley S. Klein*

For years I looked at maps and wondered when I'd finally get to Prairie Dunes Country Club. The middle of Kansas is not exactly well traveled, even among those searching for fine golf course architecture. Ever since seeing enchanting photographs of Prairie Dunes' par-4 eighth hole in Dan Jenkins's *The Best 18 Holes in America*, I knew I had to make the journey. And now, having spent two magical days there, I can honestly say that playing Prairie Dunes is a transcendent experience.

This layout became a legend while still a nine-hole course. Perry Maxwell designed the original layout that opened in 1936. His son, Press Maxwell, added nine holes in 1955. Since then the course has played host to three U.S. Women's Amateurs, a Curtis Cup, the U.S. Mid-Amateur and a U.S. Senior Amateur. Its stunning beauty soon was also on display for a national television audience for the 2002 U.S. Women's Open, won by Juli Inkster.

When the winds blow at 15-25 mph, as they are wont to do across this open grassland, scores skyrocket. Who says a course that tips out at 6,598 yards can't be a challenge today? Pure sandy links conditions prevail here in the middle of the American heartland. The fairways sit gently in the troughs of crumpled washboard land that resembles coastal dunes. The holes unfold easily, and the whole course is readily walkable.

But for all the beauty and naturalness of the landforms, the holes can play brutally tough. Credit for that goes to greens that were considered heavily undulating long before Stimpmeter speeds of nine were commonplace. Maxwell's Rolls, as they are called, live up to their reputation as maddening. At an average size of only 4,500 square feet, the greens are not easy to hit and are even harder to hold.

| | |
|---|---|
| **Par** | 70 |
| **Yards** | 6,598 |
| **Slope** | 139 |
| **Rating** | 74.0 |

**Golfweek Rating**
**8.43**

The playing areas appear generous, but they quickly take on a ferocious character, more so with wind. All fairway bunkers are positioned diagonally, leaving one side open and the other side implicated in a heightened risk/reward scenario. Bold shots are rewarded with better angles of approach—or punished with cruelty and the certain loss of a stroke.

Veteran superintendent Philip D. George, CGCS, keeps the place lean and mean. The ryegrass fairways offer lots of kick and roll. Early in the morning or late in the afternoon, shadows cast an eerie charm across the contours of this unique course, making the little hollows and swales seem as if they are rippling before one's eyes.

The powerful presence of the land also is evident in the many wildflowers and native grasses that compose the wicked roughs. Wayward shots, even those that appear to land in the first cut of rough, have a strange way of bounding two or three more times into oblivion amid knee-high thickets of big bluestem, little bluestem, Indian grass, switchgrass and sand lovegrass.

Perry Maxwell's handiwork is on wondrous display here. The holes that remain of his original work—Nos. 1-2, 6-10 and 17-18 of the present routing—offer beautiful angles of approach, shotmaking options and greens that are perfectly integrated into their surrounds. Some of the newer holes are equally compelling; there's also a stiffness and forced quality to a few of them that makes them just a tad inferior to original holes. Still, this is layout that draws one in spiritually and never for a second lets up the interest.

### America's Best: Rater's Notebook

### 1. Ease and intimacy of routing: 9
The routing wraps elegantly around the low, rambling clubhouse, with the front nine returning twice and the back nine unfolding in a large, counterclockwise loop.

### 2. Quality of feature shaping: 9
Hard to know what was built and what the Big Guy upstairs created. One of the many joys of old-style, push-up greens is that they could be seamlessly melded into the surrounding terrain without appearing awkward.

### 3. Natural setting and overall land plan: 9
A comfy fit for a totally unpretentious private club. There's a modest range shoehorned between the first and seventh holes, the 10th tee is perched on the clubhouse patio, and the second half of the par-4 18th hole ("Evening Shadow") brushes up against the clubhouse. Not a house to be spotted on site— just wavy grass, dunes and wildlife galore.

### 4. Interest of greens and surrounding contours: 9
Once the ball is on the ground, it's always moving in three dimensions, which makes the short game endlessly fascinating. Putting in the wind is tough enough, but on these greens, with banked slopes commonplace, it's even more demanding.

### 5. Variety and memorability of par 3s: 4
Original par 3s (161-yard second, 185-yard 10th) are lovely, though brutal if you miss the green. But the two newer Press Maxwell holes are a bit disappointing—uphill, awkward and uninteresting. The 168-yard fourth calls for a high cut to an unreceptive green; the 200-yard 15th ("The Chute") plays through a narrow opening of cottonwood trees (the canopies actually join limbs and interlock above the teeing ground) to a domed putting surface.

### 6. Variety and memorability of par 4s: 9
Lots of angles to play, especially at the famous eighth hole ("Dunes"), a 430-yard, uphill hole with multiple tee shot options and a green perched above a stern bunker complex. The lone anomaly is the 390-yard 12th hole, where cottonwoods occupy the landing area; the tee shot must thread the trouble and the approach has to parachute in to a tabletop green.

### 7. Variety and memorability of par 5s: 7
Good contrast, as the par 5s run in opposite directions. The 512-yard seventh is fairly simple and receptive, while the 500-yard 17th climbs relentlessly to a green that falls off sharply on both sides.

### 8. Basic quality of conditioning: 10
Amazing contrasts of playing surfaces in terms of color, texture and playing character. Course is kept dry and fast

down the middle, with green speeds held under 10. Here, well-manicured includes lots of scruffy, wild edges.

### 9. Landscape and tree management: 8

No ornamental flowerbeds or cutesy plantings. Superintendent Philip D. George, CGCS, works hard to thin out native roughs, but those cottonwoods midway on the back nine look and play like oversized darts that landed from outer space.

### 10. "Walk in the park" test: 10

By far the most compelling inland walk of any U.S. course, thanks to the dunes and a profusion of prairie animals. The course participates in an annual North American Bird Watching Open, sponsored by Audubon International, during which 40-50 species are observed on site.

**Overall vote by *Golfweek* course raters: 8.43**

| Hole | 1 | 2 | 3 | 4 | 5 | 6 | 7 | 8 | 9 | Out |
|---|---|---|---|---|---|---|---|---|---|---|
| Yardage | 432 | 161 | 355 | 168 | 438 | 387 | 512 | 430 | 426 | 3,309 |
| Par | 4 | 3 | 4 | 3 | 4 | 4 | 4 | 4 | 4 | 35 |

| Hole | 10 | 11 | 12 | 13 | 14 | 15 | 16 | 17 | 18 | In | Total |
|---|---|---|---|---|---|---|---|---|---|---|---|
| Yardage | 185 | 452 | 390 | 395 | 370 | 200 | 415 | 500 | 382 | 3,289 | 6,598 |
| Par | 3 | 4 | 4 | 4 | 4 | 3 | 4 | 5 | 4 | 35 | 70 |

Card of the Course

**Architect:** Seth Raynor, 1923    **Superintendent:** Jonathan S. Jennings, CGCS

# Chicago Golf Club

## Wheaton, Illinois

To play Chicago Golf Club is to walk in golf history, as this is one of the oldest tracks in the United States and a Parthenon of the game. The club had the first 18-hole course in America and in 1894 was one of the founding members of the U.S. Golf Association. The original layout was designed by Charles Blair Macdonald, one of the game's most celebrated architects and winner of the first U.S. Amateur. Chicago Golf, as it's called, was later revamped by Macdonald's talented protégé, Seth Raynor, who created several holes that mimic Old World classics such as the Redan and Biarritz.

Chicago has been the site of three U.S. Opens (1897, 1900, 1911) as well as four U.S. Amateurs and one Walker Cup. (A second Walker Cup is scheduled there in 2005.) But that history is only part of Chicago's allure, as it is a quiet and private nature retreat with minimal play and little fanfare. The course itself is something to behold, a masterful, links-style layout in the middle of the heartland, with generous fairways and greens, brilliant bunkering and huge swatches of field grass that turns golden yellow in the heat of the summer and sways back and forth with the afternoon winds.

It looks a little short on the card, but the first three holes quickly let you know that there is nothing easy about Chicago. No. 1 is a tough, 450-yard par 4, and the second hole is only 10 yards shorter and just as difficult. The third is an unusual, 219-yard par 3, with a deep slope traversing the approach and six ample bunkers guarding the landing area and green. Get by those holes in decent shape and you have a chance of putting together a good round.

But playing well here is less important than getting to play at all. The opportunity to experience this historic course is reason enough to celebrate. They don't make places like Chicago Golf any more.

—*John Steinbreder*

| | |
|---|---|
| **Par** | **70** |
| **Yards** | **6,574** |
| **Slope** | **130** |
| **Rating** | **72.1** |

**Golfweek Rating**
**8.37**

# Anatomy of a Green Fee

## By Scott Kauffman

Whether paying $35 to play in the heart of Orlando's summer or $250 for a round in the middle of Phoenix-Scottsdale's peak winter, golfers are accustomed to the industry's varied green fees.

Much like the airline and hotel industries, whose creative pricing practices can be difficult to comprehend, a green fee reflects a course's cost of doing business and the clientele it draws.

Regardless of region or the type of course, two underlying factors shape the establishment of a green fee: maintenance and debt service.

"Those are two of the biggest things . . . The upkeep of the course and the mortgage payment," said Tim Hartson,

Prairies Golf Club in Kalamazoo—the average annual maintenance expense is a mere $216,000 per course, almost a third of each course's average overall annual operating budget of $690,000. The biggest expense item, $231,000, at a Par 5 Golf Group course covers lease payments/debt service and management labor (superintendent's and head pro's salaries).

The other big chunk in Hartson's annual operating budget is $203,000 in administrative expenses for such items as utilities, liability insurance, employee health care, computer costs and Par 5's management fee. Throw in $40,000 in pro shop expenses, which includes hourly labor,

# "One good guideline is to charge at least $10 of green fee for every $1 million in course construction and facility development costs..."

president of Plainwell, Michigan-based Par 5 Golf Group, whose three West Michigan courses average $36 per round for green fee and cart.

At Hartson's properties—Lake Doster Golf Club in Plainwell, Wallinwood Springs Golf Club in Jenison and The

pro shop supplies and the cost of keeping handicaps, and Par 5 Golf Group knows it needs at least $690,000 in green fee revenue to break even.

Another way to look at it, according to Hartson, is his break-even cost per round—based on 20,000 full

# Cost Breakdown
## Par 5 Golf Group

rounds in 2001—is $34.50. Hartson said he actually realized an average of $36 per round for the year, conceivably earning a profit of $1.50 per golfer per round, or $30,000 total.

Hartson's figures do not include food and beverage revenues and expenses and shared labor costs between the golf operations and the food and beverage business, which are operated separately.

On the other end of the golf spectrum is semiprivate Tattersall Golf Club in West Chester, Pennsylvania, where green fees range from $88 to $108. There, the maintenance budget alone was nearly $811,000 in 2001. The overall operating budget was $1.84 million, according to Meadowbrook Golf director of marketing Mike Kelly, whose Orlando, Florida-area company manages the course.

Because Tattersall's property has greater revenue streams than Par 5's courses, the green fee model is more complex at the Philadelphia-area layout. Since Tattersall markets itself to more events such as tournaments and corporate functions, the green fee isn't based as narrowly on what the company pays for maintenance and other large administrative expenses such as taxes and insurance.

So is there a general rule the industry uses in establishing that elusive green fee?

According to many executives, one good guideline is to charge at least $10 of green fee for every $1 million in course construction and facility development costs, assuming maintenance for 40,000 rounds of golf.

The following figures were provided by Par 5 Golf Group in Plainwell, Michigan, which operates Lake Doster Golf Club, Wallinwood Springs Golf Club and The Prairies Golf Club. All figures for expenses and the breakdown of a green fee are averages of the three courses. Food and beverage costs and revenue are not included.

## Annual expenses

| | |
|---|---|
| *Maintenance* | $216,000 |
| *Pro shop* | $40,000 |
| *Administrative*★ | $203,000 |
| *Mortgage* | $231,000 |
| **Total** | **$690,000** |

★ Includes utilities, insurance, office expenses, health care, and management fees.

## Breakdown for every $36 green fee
(avg. 20,000 rounds per course)

| | |
|---|---|
| *Maintenance* | $10.80 |
| *Pro shop* | $2.00 |
| *Administrative* | $10.14 |
| *Mortgage* | $11.56 |
| **Total toward expenses** | **$34.50** |
| **Profit per golfer** | **$1.50** |

Several executives, however, take a skeptical view of such guidelines, saying golf operations can differ drastically depending on location.

"General rules of thumb can be dangerous," said Kelly, whose Meadowbrook company manages more than 100 courses nationwide. "Only because if you don't analyze all the facts of your market, you can position course 'A' too high or course 'B' too low.

"You have to do a feasibility study of the demographics and competitive analysis to determine what the market is. Then you have to determine what niche you have. It's a constant process. The landscape changes with every golf course that comes on board."

Take a desert state such as Arizona, where water is a precious commodity. Richard Singer, director of consulting services for the National Golf Foundation, says he calculates at least $20 per golfer per round to pay for water rights. And that doesn't include the cost of pumping the water.

In the harsh desert climate of Phoenix-Scottsdale, for example, green fees can't be under $30-$40, "unless you were a municipal operation," Singer said. "Some may spend $10 a round on water, some may spend 38 cents. It's very local, very site specific."

There are so many variables from facility type to facility type, he added, that a green fee model "just doesn't exist."

M. G. Orender, president of the PGA of America and proprietor of a Jacksonville, Florida-based management firm called Hampton Golf, offers some advice for Florida and other locales where golf is played year-round. Orender uses the following numbers as good operational benchmarks for a typical $6 million course that is positioned in the upper-middle to high-end daily-fee market: If the course has a moderate-size clubhouse (6,000-8,000 square feet), staffs bag drops, starters and rangers, it will have an estimated operating budget of $1.4 million to $1.7 million. Of that total, maintenance accounts for 32 percent to 35 percent of the total, general administration such as insurance and property taxes is 25 percent to 30 percent, food and beverage costs, including wages for cooks and wait staff, run 10 percent to 15 percent, and outside services such as starters, rangers and "cart jockeys" comprise eight percent to 10 percent.

Throw in an additional $600,000 in debt service, and the typical warm-season course operating at the $1.7 million level is now at $2.3 million in expenses, and that's before cost of goods sold (estimated $200,000-plus) and capital expenditures for golf carts and turf maintenance equipment (estimated $100,000-plus) are factored in.

Normally, a facility will target about 10 percent profit on course operations alone. "The bottom line is I need 'X' number of rounds to keep the ship floating," said Orender.

Keeping the ship afloat is easier said than done, especially in the highly competitive Florida market. For example, if a course handles 38,000 rounds per year, that facility needs to book about 10,000 rounds during the three peak winter months (January-March) at $75 per head ($750,000 in total green fee revenue), 26,000 rounds during the rest of the year at $45 ($1,170,000) and another 2,000 rounds during the afternoon hours at $40 ($80,000). That adds up to $2 million in total green fee revenue.

"If you're operating at $1.4 million, you might have made your debt service," said Orender, who has been involved in managing more than 50 courses in 11 different states. "If you're operating at $1.7 million, well . . ."

The ship might be taking on water—or needing to offload ballast in the form of personnel, service or conditioning.

In either case, someone is going to pay. If it's not the owner, it's going to be the golfer.

## Tattersall Golf Club

Tattersall Golf Club is a fairly new semiprivate course in the Philadelphia area. Its green fees range from $88 to $108. Below is the course's operating budget for 2001. A breakdown of the green fee was unavailable.

| Expense | Amount | Budget % |
|---|---|---|
| Pro shop labor | $183,696 | 9.97% |
| Food & beverage labor | $7,500 | .41% |
| Course maintenance labor | $358,659 | 19.47% |
| Marketing labor | $27,807 | 1.51% |
| Administrative labor | $55,462 | 3.01% |
| Pro shop expense | $64,196 | 3.48% |
| Food & beverage expense | $299* | .02% |
| Course maintenance | $452,077 | 24.54% |
| Marketing expense | $50,884 | 2.76% |
| Administrative expense | $429,039 | 23.29% |
| Other | $212,630 | 11.54% |
| **Total** | **$1,842,249** | **100%** |

* Course was operating a hot dog concession stand while restaurant was being built.

**Architects:** Donald J. Ross, 1929 • Dick Wilson, 1947   **Superintendent:** Harold Hicks

# Seminole Golf Club

## North Palm Beach, Florida

Seminole is a bastion of tradition. Open for play from October through April only, this Donald Ross gem is the understated winter home for dozens of movers and shakers in the U.S. Golf Association. The season-ending George Coleman Invitational annually attracts the game's top career amateurs to Seminole.

Spending time in the locker room and perusing the club's scrapbooks may be as big a treat as playing the course. Ben Hogan practiced here in the weeks leading up to the Masters each spring. Claude Harmon, winner of the 1948 Masters, was head pro here in the winter and head pro at Winged Foot in the summer. These days, that position is held by Bob Ford, who summers at Oakmont.

Seminole's layout, hard by the Atlantic, is notable for its variety of green complexes, its multitude of bunkers and scruffy waste areas, and the pace of its routing—especially the four holes that utilize the sand ridge that separates the course from the beach. Some architecture critics contend that much of Ross' original sculpting was destroyed when Dick Wilson secretly rebuilt the course after World War II.

A great deal of Seminole's character, however, was restored by Brian Silva in 1996.

Wind is always a factor; when it blows hard and the greens are shaved, Seminole is a beast. So be it. If you're lucky enough to be invited to play Seminole, don't fixate on your score. Just savor the experience.

—*Dave Seanor*

| | |
|---|---|
| **Par** | 72 |
| **Yards** | 6,836 |
| **Slope** | 143 |
| **Rating** | 73.6 |

**Golfweek Rating**
**8.32**

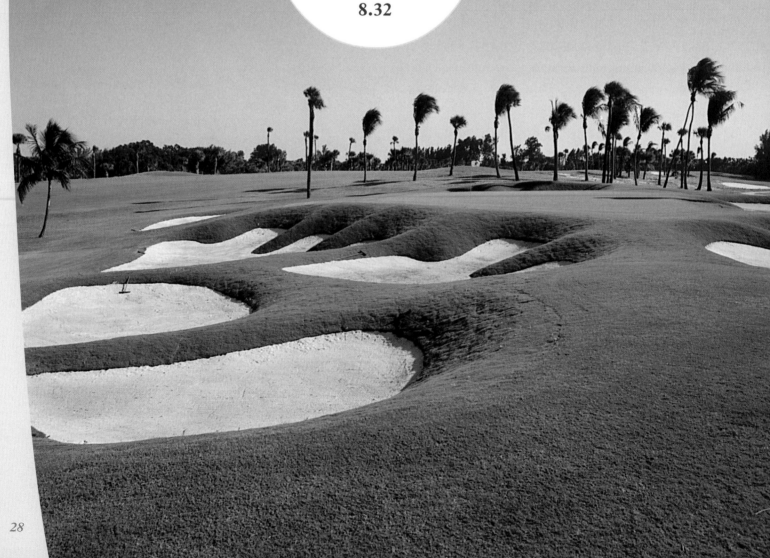

**Architect:** A. W. Tillinghast, 1923     **Superintendent:** Joseph Eric Greytok

# Winged Foot Golf Club (West)

## Mamaroneck, New York

Five U.S. Opens, with another on the way in 2006; the U.S. Amateur in 1940, with another coming in 2004; the Walker Cup in 1949; the PGA Championship in 1997.

Winged Foot West is where the history of championship golf comes to life on one of the game's sternest tests. When Mark Brooks was defending his PGA championship in '97, he said of Winged Foot West: "There are about six hard holes out here, six very hard holes and six impossible holes."

Perhaps Brooks was dabbling in melodrama, but his point is well taken. A round at Winged Foot West is a constant battle, requiring long, accurate tee shots through trees and controlled, long-iron approaches to bunkered, sloping greens. Need concrete proof of the difficulty? When Hale Irwin won the 1974 U.S. Open at Winged Foot West, his score was 7 over par.

The course is not only demanding, but it departs from one of golf architecture's most stringent rules—that a great piece of land is a prerequisite for having a great course. Winged Foot is laid out over rather ordinary (but wonderfully maintained) terrain, yet it is A. W. Tillinghast's masterpiece.

Primary examples of Tillinghast's genius are No. 3, a 215-yard par 3; the signature 10th hole, a 190-yard par 3; No. 14, a 440-yard par 4; No. 15, a 415-yard par 4; and a classic picture in American golf, the 450-yard par-4 18th.

*—Jeff Barr*

| Par | 72 |
| --- | --- |
| **Yards** | **6,956** |
| **Slope** | **140** |
| **Rating** | **73.2** |

***Golfweek* Rating**
**8.17**

*Classic* course profile

**Architects:** Devereux Emmett, 1901 • Walter Travis, 1926    **Superintendent:** Ed Butler

# The Garden City Golf Club

## Garden City, New York

Much history has been recorded on the 160 acres composing Garden City Golf Club. The modest clubhouse on Stewart Avenue faces a busy, if not elegant, metropolitan New York suburb. Inside, under a vaulted ceiling, is one of golf's great locker rooms. This is very much a men's club (jacket and tie required), though the dress code is considerably more relaxed once you head onto the golf course.

Garden City Golf, as it's called, is one of the game's storied layouts, having played host to, among other events, the 1902 U.S. Open, the 1924 Walker Cup and four U.S. Amateurs, the last in 1937.

The opening hole, a 302-yard par 4 with a massive, scratchy old cross bunker to contend with, sets the tone for the day. It looks like something out of a P. G. Wodehouse novel and plays about as maddeningly. The sandy loam soil is ideal for fast golf, and while the fairways are fairly wide, there are plenty of deep, punitive bunkers and knee-high fescue roughs snagging off-line shots.

Throughout the round, golfers confront a strange mix of the quirky and the bold. As if in defiance of modern conventions until the end, Garden City Golf ends with a par 3—the first of three on our top 50 classical list to do so, including Cascades (No. 39) and East Lake (No. 44).

—*Bradley S. Klein*

| | |
|---|---|
| **Par** | **73** |
| **Yards** | **6,911** |
| **Slope** | **139** |
| **Rating** | **73.8** |

***Golfweek* Rating**
**8.14**

# The Value of a Good Superintendent

## By Bradley S. Klein

Back in the 1960s, Bethpage State Park's Black Course in Farmingdale, N.Y., looked like a beat-up muni. Everyone on Long Island knew it had a strong routing and some character to the fairways and greens. But turfgrass cover was thin and spotty, weeds abounded and tees were beaten up.

Fast-forward to June 2002.

To those who grew up scraping the ball around "The Black," coming to its reincarnation into a host site for the U.S. Open was like stepping into a dream world. Credit for the transformation goes, in part, to a major investment by

noticed, publicized and appreciated. During the U.S. Open, Currier went into the media tent with USGA championship agronomist Tim Moraghan and held a news conference where they fielded technical questions about course setup and greens conditions

Most golfers don't bother to speak with their home course superintendent and probably don't even know his— or her—name. That's because too many people take for granted the importance of course conditioning and only speak up when they have a complaint. That's too bad. Unless they have a good relationship with their greenkeeper and

## "For years, superintendents were considered on par with the local village idiot and treated accordingly."

the U.S. Golf Association and architect Rees Jones. But much of the praise rightly has been directed at Bethpage State Park's golf course superintendent, Craig Currier, and to his entire crew.

For folks in the golf business, the attention on a superintendent's work has been long overdue. For years, greenkeepers stayed in the background. But now, in part thanks to expanded media coverage that includes specialized golf magazines and a dedicated cable TV channel, the behind-the-scenes work of folks such as Currier is getting

understand, or at least appreciate, the value of good maintenance, there's a fair chance their own concerns with the golf course won't be taken seriously. Moreover, golfers who know even a little about what it takes to maintain a golf course actually can enjoy their rounds more and improve their play by a few strokes each round.

For years, superintendents were considered on par with the local village idiot and treated accordingly. They often looked and dressed like farmers and were relegated to a barn on the far end of the property. Of

Early morning on a golf course, the loveliest time of day.

Kip Tyler (CGCS, Salem Country Club, Peabody, Ma.), was voted "Superintendent of the Year" for 2001 by Golfweek's *SuperNews*.

Machines and hand labor are needed to get bunkers ready.

Changing cups, one of many daily rituals that are part of basic greenkeeping.

course, those were the days when fairways and tees were mowed once a week with a horse-drawn reel mower and when the standard arsenal of golf course chemicals consisted of arsenic, seaweed and dried cattle blood. Then along came full-length irrigation systems, the Stimpmeter, the Environmental Protection Administration and computerized spreadsheet budgeting. That's when greenkeepers abandoned their reputation as demented field hands and became scientifically trained turfgrass managers.

The shift in conditioning from the classical era to modern golf has been simply amazing. If they had been able to measure green speeds in the 1920s, all of those wonderful old putting greens would have registered about 5 or 6 on the Stimpmeter. Bunkers were only occasionally raked. Fairway lies regularly caused flyers. And during the middle of the day you had to stick a 4-iron into one of those surface watering values that went "pffft, pffft, pffft" if you wanted to play an approach shot from the fairway.

Today, greenkeepers do their watering at night, rake the bunkers every day, and not only mow greens as tight as 1/10th of an inch in height but also groom them with special rollers to eliminate grain. No wonder you'll find many clubs today whose scorecards list the superintendent along with the course architect and PGA club professional. Finally, belatedly, superintendents are getting the credit they deserve.

# Kip Tyler's Year of Living Dangerously

It was a year like no other of the 20 seasons that Kip Tyler, CGCS, has spent tending the fairways and greens of Salem Country Club in Peabody, Massachusetts, the 42nd ranked course on our Classic list. The litany of troubles he faced looks like the 10 plagues of the Old Testament. Here's what he had to deal with leading into, during and immediately following the 2001 U.S. Senior Open. It's also why Tyler's efforts earned him recognition as Superintendent of the Year by "*Golfweek*'s SuperNews" for 2001.

**Dec. 30, 2000**—Two inches of slush freezes, leading to hockey rink conditions on black ice covering fairways.

**Jan. 7-17, 2001**—Snowblower removes snow cover on 10 greens.

**Feb. 3, 2001**—Tyler measures 28 inches of snow cover on golf course.

**March 1, 2001**—Jackhammers, snowblower and front-end loaders are used to dislodge six inches of ice, revealing vast patches of devastated turf.

**May 19, 2001**—Gas line cracks on a greens mower, leaving three trails of dead grass on ninth green (tournament routing).

**May 22, 2001**—Gas leak on a greens mower leaves trail of damage across 12th green.

**May 25, 2001**—Sixteen holes reopen for member play, but vandals steal 12 flags and damage first and fourth greens.

**May 26, 2001**—Blown hydraulic oil hose on fairway mower leaves four-inch-wide line of dead grass down sixth fairway.

**June 6, 2001**—Veteran full-time crew member suddenly leaves staff to take "dream job" in local municipality.

**June 10, 2001**—At 2 a.m., a pump house electric power line explodes underground, leaving the course without irrigation and wilting for a day; United Rental Co., on site installing tents, saves Salem for a week with a temporary generator.

**June 12-14, 2001**—Veteran mechanic Richard Selvo forced to sit out work because of potentially fatal case of cellulitis in infected foot.

**June 18, 2001**—Crew member rolls triplex mower down side of practice tee newly built for the Senior Open; emergency rescue vehicles cause damage to practice area while saving him.

**June 28, 2001**—First round of 2001 U.S. Senior Open.

**June 30, 2001**—Torrential storm on afternoon of third round brings play to halt as two inches of rain flood course; lightning strike knocks out TV tower and 28 television sets on the grounds; irrigation pipe gets blown out of the ground; exiting fans body-surf down fairways.

**July 1, 2001**—Little time for morning preparation owing to resumption of third round early Sunday with players shotgunning on the last seven holes at 7 a.m., plus fourth-round tee times assigned to both nines immediately afterward.

**July 2, 2001**—"Morning after" double shotgun (7:30 a.m./1 p.m.) to accommodate corporate sponsors.

**July 3, 2001**—Salem Country Club closed. Crew sleeps in.

*ClassicCourseFeature*

# Los Angeles Country Club (North)

## Los Angeles, California

The 315 acres composing the Los Angeles Country Club might be the most valuable real estate in golf. The location is impressive enough—straddling Beverly Hills and within earshot of Sunset Boulevard. Small wonder that any house you spot immediately around the club's grounds is valued at upward of $6 million. Among the more noteworthy residences adjoining the golf holes are the Playboy Mansion and the former Guggenheim Estate (now home to singer Lionel Ritchie).

For all the opulence in the area, LACC manages to maintain a low profile. This is not the golf club in town for Hollywood celebrities. No, this is an old-fashioned place, with a sprawling Southern colonial clubhouse that's home to elegant dining rooms and museum-quality golf memorabilia. Much of the history on display was made right outside on the club's two 1920s-vintage layouts, the North and South courses.

LACC's legendary North Course is a collaborative effort of the West Coast's premier designers from the golden age of golf design. The team of George C. Thomas Jr. and William P. Bell completed fewer than a dozen layouts in their heyday of the 1920s. That portfolio includes such stylish courses as Riviera Country Club in Pacific Palisades (No. 25 Classical), Bel-Air Country Club in Los Angeles and Stanford Golf Club in Palo Alto.

Thomas and Bell had a knack for routings that maximized native features such as dry washes. On the North Course, they managed to create great strategic diversity despite an elevation change on site of 140 feet. Several tee shots require a carry across deep gullies to reach level ground on the far side. Rarely is the line of play perpendicular to such native landforms; it's almost always arrayed diagonally to maximize the sense of strategic angle.

| Par | 71 |
|---|---|
| **Yards** | 6,909 |
| **Slope** | 135 |
| **Rating** | 74.0 |

***Golfweek* Rating**
**8.07**

Their bunkers had a scratched-out look. A recent restoration overseen by John Harbottle has strengthened the depth and visual impact of the original bunker shapes, though in the process the old scruffiness of the place has been modernized. Years of tree overgrowth have closed down some of the alternative play paths, but with the holes winding across rolling land and calling for shots that traverse attractive dry washes, golfers continually are treated to a fascinating set of demands and need to be able to work the ball both ways in order to secure the ideal line of approach.

The par 3s are a particular thrill, with driver the popular club of choice at the 244-yard 11th, a reverse Redan that plays into a backdrop of downtown L.A. The 133-yard 15th, by contrast, calls for a delicate little lob shot to a banana-shaped putting surface. It was here in 1962 that a foursome registered the amazing score of 1-1-2-2.

## America's Best: Rater's Notebook

### 1. Ease and intimacy of routing: 10

Course unfolds easily from the clubhouse, with front nine making a tight counterclockwise loop and the back nine ambling about in the rough. In classic golden era form, the tees tend to sit on the near side of deep swales, with play across them on the drive.

### 2. Integrity of original design: 6

Basic hole corridors remain from the 1927 version of LACC-North, though the search for more yardage in the early 1980s

led to three greens on front side (Nos. 2, 6, 8) being moved back some 40 yards each. Initially discordant putting surfaces here have since been resolved through stylistic integration as part of late 1990s renovation.

## 3. Natural setting and overall land plan: 8

Staid elegance of the club grounds comport well with surrounding residential areas.

## 4. Interest of greens and surrounding contours: 8

The Greens' character is derived from dramatic dominant slopes that are very hard to read. The greens, averaging 6,000 square feet, are planted in relatively quick A-4 bentgrass; chipping to them from thick, common Bermuda-grass rough makes for something of a guessing game.

## 5. Variety and memorability of par 3s: 10

The variety comes not only in distances but also in types of terrain and shape of required shot. Front nine presents a dramatically downhill, medium-length fourth, the long level seventh and the slightly uphill medium-length ninth. Back nine par 3s are even more contrasting, with 111 yards of distance differentiating the two par 3s and the greens shaped in opposite ways.

## 6. Variety and memorability of par 4s: 7

Good fairway movement and variety of terrain, though shot-making options are limited by tree overgrowth. The option of going for the green on the short sixth was taken away in early 1980s when the green was pushed back, so that the hole is now basically a mandatory layup. Longer par 4s on back are especially strong, with exception of 18th.

## 7. Variety and memorability of par 5s: 6

First three par 5s are modest and not especially compelling, but the 14th hole is truly inspired, with switchback shots required on drive and second, and the green is beautifully defended and very hard to hold.

## 8. Basic quality of conditioning: 8

Solid throughout. Kudos to the club and to superintendent Bruce Williams, CGCS, for their commitment to firm and fast conditions, including dormant common Bermuda grass in winter.

## 9. Landscape and tree management: 4

Indigenous California sycamore in barrancas help define those low areas, but proliferation of eucalyptus and pine has cluttered some playing corridors and limited strategic options.

## 10. "Walk in the park" test: 9

A gracious place, easy to walk and enjoyable all the way. Course is the best part, but looking at some of those adjoining enhances one's sense of looking behind the scenes at a substantial community.

**Overall vote by *Golfweek* course raters: 8.07**

| Hole | 1 | 2 | 3 | 4 | 5 | 6 | 7 | 8 | 9 | Out | |
|---|---|---|---|---|---|---|---|---|---|---|---|
| Yardage | 524 | 543 | 385 | 207 | 478 | 340 | 233 | 561 | 177 | 3,448 | Card of the Course |
| Par | 5 | 5 | 4 | 3 | 4 | 4 | 3 | 5 | 3 | 36 | |
| Hole | 10 | 11 | 12 | 13 | 14 | 15 | 16 | 17 | 18 | In | Total |
| Yardage | 374 | 244 | 368 | 453 | 564 | 133 | 447 | 432 | 446 | 3,461 | 6,909 |
| Par | 4 | 3 | 4 | 4 | 5 | 3 | 4 | 4 | 4 | 35 | 71 |

**Architects:** Donald J. Ross, 1918 • Robert Trent Jones Sr., 1950    **Superintendent:** Steven Cook, CGCS

# Oakland Hills
# Country Club (South)

## Birmingham, Michigan

| Par | 72 |
| --- | --- |
| Yards | 7,105 |
| Slope | 137 |
| Rating | 75.5 |

**Golfweek Rating**
**8.03**

Donald Ross formulated this masterpiece in 1918, but it was Robert Trent Jones Sr. who created a monster.

After Jones conducted the first of his three renovations in 1950 (the other two—far more minor—came in 1972 and '84), Ben Hogan proclaimed his joy at bringing "this course, this monster, to its knees" during his 1951 U.S. Open victory at Oakland Hills. It has been The Monster ever since.

Virtually every hole has played host to history—from David Graham's 4-iron to the par-3 third hole that set up a winning eight-foot birdie putt in a playoff against Ben Crenshaw in the 1979 PGA Championship, to Gary Player's majestic shot over a willow tree and pond on the 16th to win the PGA in 1972, to Davis Love III's three-putt on the final hole of the 1996 U.S. Open.

No. 16, a 406-yard, dogleg-right par 4 with the second shot over a pond, has become the South Course's signature hole. But it isn't the toughest. That distinction belongs to No. 14, a 473-yard par 4 that appears deceptively serene. There are no bunkers to deal with off the tee, but it's a long hole that gets tougher down the fairway. And the 14th green is nasty, particularly if there's a pin placement at the front right of the putting surface. Other highlights include the par-3, 171-yard 13th and the 423-yard, par-4 11th.

History, difficulty and elegance. You decide. Masterpiece or monster?

—*Jeff Barr*

# The Olympic Club (Lake)

## San Francisco, California

Many players have likened the challenge of The Olympic Club to playing in a wind tunnel. Towering pines, cypress, cedar, redwood and eucalyptus trees encroach on nearly every fairway, demanding superior accuracy off the tee. All were planted after the course was built on sand dunes, a half-mile from the Pacific Ocean.

The Lake Course has played host to four U.S. Opens—Jack Fleck stunned Ben Hogan there in 1955, and Billy Casper caught an overconfident Arnold Palmer to win in 1966—and two U.S. Amateurs. The view of San Francisco

| | |
|---|---|
| **Par** | 71 |
| **Yards** | 6,826 |
| **Slope** | 126 |
| **Rating** | 72.8 |

**Golfweek Rating**

**8.01**

and the Golden Gate Bridge from the tee at No. 3 may be Olympic's most memorable feature, but from a strategic outlook, its varied and demanding par 4s—particularly Nos. 4 and 5—are what set the course apart.

There are no water hazards on the Lake Course at Olympic, and only one fairway bunker. But because of San Francisco's moist air, the layout typically plays longer than its 6,826 yards.

**—Dave Seanor**

39

**Architects:** A. W. Tillinghast & Joe Burbeck, 1935    **Superintendent:** Craig Currier

# Bethpage State Park (Black)

## Farmingdale, New York

*Classic course profile*

Bethpage Black found itself at the center of a New York lovefest during the 2002 U.S. Open.

Tiger Woods won the tournament, but the star was a municipal layout that already had been the stuff of urban legend. For decades, avid public links golfers would sleep in their cars all night in the parking lot just to get a tee time—and a six-hour round of golf. Now the whole world knows what the hubbub was about, and the USGA, to its credit, already has decided to bring the Open back in 2009.

The course has it all—dramatic diagonal bunkers in landing areas, deep greenside bunkers, four-inch bluegrass rough and greens that putt a lot more dangerously than they look. For years, the big drawback to Bethpage Black was lousy conditioning—a problem shared by the park's four other 18-hole layouts.

That changed in the late 1990s after the USGA invested $3 million in the course and the New York State Department of Parks, Recreation and Historic Preservation, which owns the course, put more money into maintenance. By U.S. Open week, the greens were in perfect shape and the world's best players loved it—even if reaching some fairways required carries of 250 yards or more. For everyday players, the course plays a little tamer. At a cost of less than $40 for state residents, Bethpage Black is the best deal in golf.

—*Bradley S. Klein*

| | |
|---|---|
| **Par** | **71** |
| **Yards** | **7,065** |
| **Slope** | **139** |
| **Rating** | **73.6** |

*Golfweek* **Rating**

**7.97**

# Wannamoisett Country Club

## Rumford, Rhode Island

| Par | 69 |
|---|---|
| Yards | 6,688 |
| Slope | 133 |
| Rating | 72.1 |

*Golfweek* **Rating**
**7.93**

The most distinctive set of greens Donald Ross ever built can be found on the west side of Providence, R.I., at Wannamoisett Country Club. The course is virtually shoehorned into a site so intimate that some back tees literally back up against the perimeter fencing. Ross thought enough of the place that he wrote to his engineer, "This is the best layout I ever made, a fine course on 100 acres, no congestion, fine variety."

Wannamoisett has a glorious championship history, starting with the 1931 PGA Championship (won by Tom Creavy). Since 1963, the course has been the site of the Northeast Amateur, which annually draws one of the strongest fields in amateur golf and has been won by the likes of Ben Crenshaw, Scott Hoch, John Cook, Hal Sutton and David Duval.

The par-69 layout calls for nervy approaches to amazingly diverse bentgrass/poa annua greens. False fronts, punchbowls, reverse slopes, domed greens—they all can be found here. There also is no shortage of cross bunkers to deal with off the tee, many of them taking away the advantage of long hitters. Position always is critical on these tree-lined holes, but nothing is tougher than keeping the golf ball on these greens—or reading them once you get there.

*—Bradley S. Klein*

**Architects:** Willie Campbell, 1895 • Howard C. Toomey & William S. Flynn, 1931   **Superintendent:** William Spence

# The Country Club (Composite)

## Brookline, Massachusetts

*Classic course profile*

| Par | 71 |
|---|---|
| **Yards** | **7,033** |
| **Slope** | **139** |
| **Rating** | **74.3** |

***Golfweek* Rating**

**7.87**

The 1988 U.S. Open at The Country Club had architectural significance far beyond the immediate moment of the event, won by Curtis Strange. The week saw the career of Rees Jones skyrocket, in large part because of his sensitive restoration of this historic course. The work not only brought back decades-old mounds, hole placements and bunkers that had become obscured or altered over the years, it also showed the world's finest players (and an international television audience) the value of traditional design.

The Country Club's rocky outcrops and gnarly native roughs have been confronting golfers for more than a century at this site. The layout has changed considerably since young amateur Francis Ouimet won the 1913 U.S. Open here, capturing the public's imagination and increasing golf's popularity in the United States. The Toomey and Flynn version makes masterful use of intriguing ground. The 451-yard par-4 third snakes through rolling terrain and demands shots that sidestep ominous cross bunkers. There's much excitement for those who go for broke at two nearly drivable par 4s on the front nine. Interestingly enough, at the 1999 Ryder Cup here, more birdies were made by players who laid up on these holes than by those who chose full-bore drivers.

The most elegant hole is the 370-yard par-4 17th, a little dogleg left around a corner bunker complex. Ouimet locked up his 1913 playoff victory against Ted Ray and Harry Vardon with a birdie here. In 1988, Curtis Strange three-putted the 17th hole from 15 feet to fall into a tie with Nick Faldo—whom he beat the next day. And at that riotous '99 Ryder Cup, all hell broke loose on the 17th green when Justin Leonard sank a 40-foot birdie putt that sealed the greatest team comeback in Ryder Cup history.

*—Bradley S. Klein*

# Southern Hills Country Club

## Tulsa, Oklahoma

An anomaly as a championship course built during the Great Depression, Southern Hills has played host to six national championships, including three U.S. Opens and two PGA Championships. It's a track for straight hitters; otherwise there's hell to pay in its wiry Bermuda-grass rough.

Southern Hills was the beneficiary of a restoration by architect Keith Foster in 1999 and 2000. Using vintage aerial photography as his guide, Foster expanded Southern Hills' greens to their original sizes. "Maxwell's greens fall back to front as well as side to side, so having those marginal areas back in play created some really good hole placements," says Foster.

The challenge of Southern Hills comes from its shifting terrain, with fairways that tip away from the line of play and leave awkward lies for approach and recovery. The par-4 18th, which played 466 yards for the 2001 U.S. Open, is as tough as they come. It is bisected by a creek and two bunkers, with golfers facing a long approach from a downhill lie to an elevated green that's flanked by bunkers and features a spoon-shaped false front.

Southern Hills is at its best in late spring and early autumn. In between, the withering heat can take its toll—on golfers and the course.

—*Dave Seanor*

| | |
|---|---|
| **Par** | **70** |
| **Yards** | **6,931** |
| **Slope** | **136** |
| **Rating** | **74.0** |

***Golfweek* Rating**
**7.81**

**Architects:** George C. Thomas Jr. & William P. Bell, 1927    **Superintendent:** Matthew Morton

# Riviera Country Club

## Pacific Palisades, California

| | |
|---|---|
| **Par** | 72 |
| **Yards** | 7,171 |
| **Slope** | 137 |
| **Rating** | 75.6 |

**Golfweek Rating**

**7.80**

In 1925, the Los Angeles Athletic Club bought 270 acres in San Monica because its members had long craved a venue where they could play golf. Within two years the result was tony Riviera, built at the bottom of a large canyon and below a majestic clubhouse.

Riviera would become known for its celebrity members and its tournament history. It also would become known as Hogan's Alley because of the feats of Ben Hogan, who won two Los Angeles Opens and a U.S. Open there in 1947-48. Riviera also was the scene of Hogan's return from a near-fatal car crash—he lost to Sam Snead in a 1950 L.A. Open playoff. The club has been home to 42 regular PGA Tour events (now called the Nissan Open) and also was the site of the 1983 and 1995 PGA Championships.

Though there's little elevation change between Nos. 1 and 18, Riviera is a collection of interesting holes that will challenge all skill levels. Holes are framed by eucalyptus trees and high cliffs; strategically placed bunkers challenge both tee shots and approaches; and Velcro-like Kikuyu grass penalizes shots that find the rough. A balanced layout—some trouble left, some trouble right—demands that players work the ball left and right and puts a premium on placement.

The natural amphitheater setting at 18 provides a dramatic view and one of the best spectator holes in golf. The risk-reward short par-4 10th, with a well-bunkered, tilted green, can yield an eagle or double bogey. The famed 170-yard sixth features a doughnut-shaped green with a bunker in the middle. And the narrow par-4 seventh once drew this question from Lee Trevino: "What happened to the other half of the fairway?"

*—Jeff Rude*

# Rediscovering the Lost Art of Strategy

## By Bradley S. Klein

I'm continually amazed and disappointed to see how few golfers know how to play strategically. Perhaps they think issues of course design are merely academic topics, to be studied in books or only at the game's legendary classical layouts. Such golfers—the bulk of middle- and high-handicappers, as far as I can tell—cheat themselves badly, and their games suffer as a result.

Golfers rarely take the time to look at a golf hole and to think through where their ball ought to be hit. Instead, their concerns seem to be more focused on swing mechanics. To the extent that they worry where the ball is going to go, it appears their primary concern is that it travel as far as possible. So instead of thinking about golf as a form of billiards, replete with angles and setup shots, they construe the game as a form of aerial bombardment in which the object is simply to hit it as far as possible.

There's one other curious element. Golfers as a group tend to think of the game in categories derived not from their own playing ability but from what they see on TV from watching the PGA Tour. Even bogey golfers tend to think of a 375-yard par-4 as short, or they'll dismiss a course that plays 6,500 yards from the back tee as being of inferior character. The strangest example of this comes from my many encounters with women's groups at private clubs.

There it's common to hear 30-handicappers praise their layout that plays 6,200 yards from the forward tees and how they love the challenge of their par 3s that all play more than 150 yards. What challenge, I wonder, can it be to go an entire golf season without once hitting a green in regulation?

There is a male counterpart to this, in the guise of the testosterone-overcharged player who insists on playing a course from the back tees, just as the pros do. But then PGA Tour pros don't play a 440-yard par 4 with a driver, topped 5-wood, 7-iron and pitching wedge.

If you really want to see the entire course, better to putt out those two-footers than to concede them.

When standing in the fairway 250 yards from the green on a par 5, the vast majority of golfers will take out a 3-wood and try to beat it onto the green. Now add a bunker or two fronting the putting surface, and all of a sudden the odds of pulling off the shot disappear to near zero. Rare is the golfer who, considering his options, will opt for a 6- or 7-iron, leaving a solid wedge in. Is that chickening out? Or simply playing smart?

Even if you hit the 3-wood well, the odds are you'll be left with either a bunker shot or an awkward half-wedge—both notoriously tough shots for most golfers. And that's if you hit the fairway wood well. The odds are probably far better for most golfers that by laying up and leaving themselves a full short-iron, they can get the ball closer in two shots than if they opted for the 3-wood. It's simply a matter of basic math so that the shots add up to 250.

Unfortunately, most golfers see it as a test of their ego, and they unnecessarily run up high scores in the process.

Small wonder that when David Toms is trying to clinch the 2001 PGA Championship at the Atlanta Athletic Club with a par 4 on the last hole and lays up short of the pond fronting the green, he gets second-guessed for not trying to win in style. Imagine the firestorm if he had missed the nine-foot putt and gone on to lose in a playoff to Phil Mickelson.

Guess what? Toms still would have made the right choice, because at the time the layup from the right rough made the most sense.

Golfers also could benefit from learning not to shoot at pins, especially those placed on the edge of putting surfaces. Instead of playing for pins tucked over bunkers or alongside ponds, most players would shoot better scores if they simply played for the front third of every green. They would give themselves a bigger cushion to miss the shot without risking hazards or other troubles.

Scratch golfers who hit the ball accurately to a predictable distance can fly at pins—at their peril.

But for most golfers, being anywhere near the middle or front of the green—regardless of hole placement—is a very comfortable place.

I'm not suggesting to never take risks. The point is to evaluate options and pick those that make sense while minimizing unnecessary, or unproductive, risks. If most golfers prefer to try shots they can't pull off, that might be because the game offers them an inconsequential way of going to extremes that is in contrast to their (mundane) workaday lives. After all, there's nothing really to be afraid of—except for losing a shot or two and a $4 golf ball.

Recklessness can be emotionally rewarding. Some golfers get more psychic gain by succeeding one-tenth of the time than by never trying at all. But there are other ways to play as well, including strategically. The boldest moves aren't always the wisest. In this sense, the course might be best thought of not as a battlefield but as a chessboard.

# "Most players would shoot better scores if they simply played for the front third of every green."

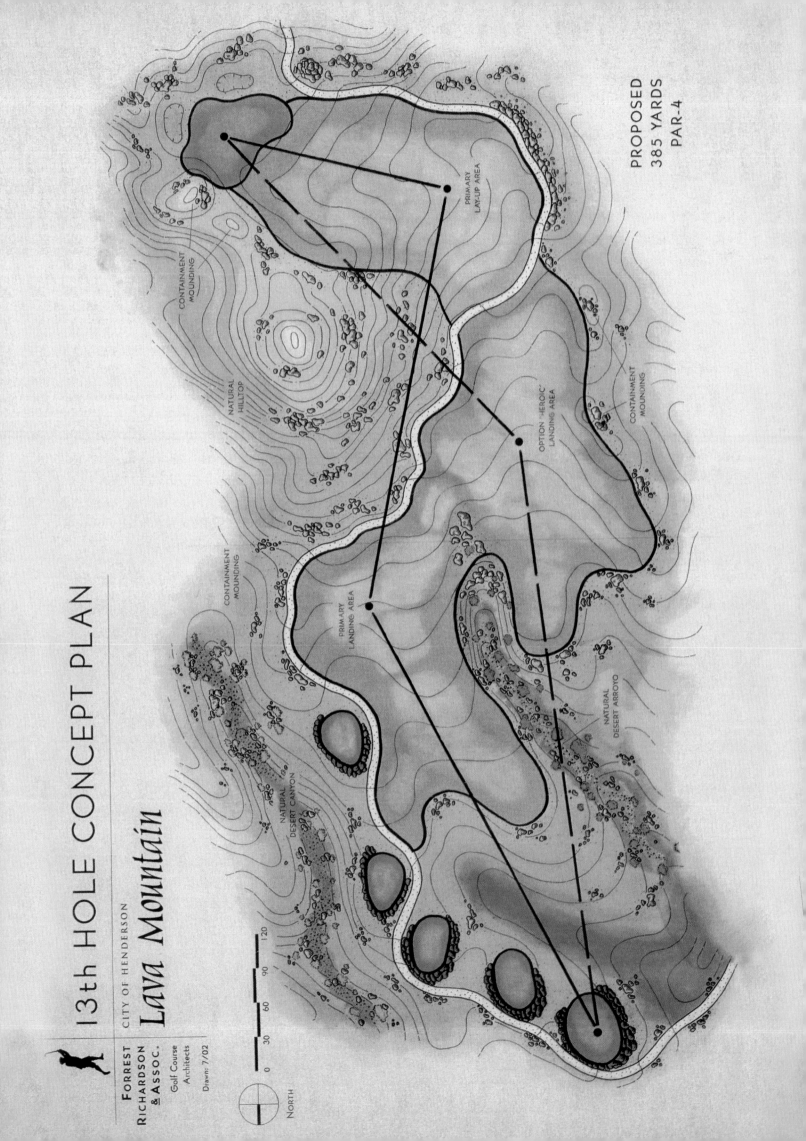

*Architect:* Seth Raynor, 1925   *Superintendent:* Douglas Norwell

# Camargo Club

## Indian Hill, Ohio

Seth Raynor (1874-1926) was a civil engineer by trade. He came to golf design secondhand through his association with Charles Blair Macdonald as a surveyor. Not a golfer and never a student of the classic British holes as his mentor was, Raynor nonetheless proved very strong in sizing up land, routing holes and getting them to fit the land.

That's the overriding strength of Camargo, one of his last projects. It often has been said of Raynor that he only had about 22 holes in mind that he could build and it was simply a matter of which 18 of them you'd get on your golf course.

All of Raynor's favorite par-3 prototypes are here: the 179-yard fifth is a more steeply sloped version of the

Eden, based on the 11th at St. Andrews. The 227-yard eighth is a bold version of the original Biarritz hole from France, complete with a deep swale through the middle and squared-off bunkers paralleling the green. The 140-yard 11th is a typical "Short" hole based upon the original at Royal West Norwalk in England. And the 192-yard 16th is a typical Redan hole, derived from North Berwick in Scotland.

Raynor favored a linear form to his feature work. Perhaps it was the civil engineer in him that opted for efficiency rather than ornateness. Whatever the motivation, Camargo, a very private club on Cincinnati's east side, embodies all of the solidity that made Raynor one of the game's enduring master builders.

—*Bradley S. Klein*

| | |
|---|---|
| **Par** | **70** |
| **Yards** | **6,588** |
| **Slope** | **133** |
| **Rating** | **72.5** |

**Golfweek Rating**

**7.75**

# Quaker Ridge Golf Club

## Scarsdale, New York

Quaker Ridge looks very different than its neighbor across the street, Winged Foot. That course has raised greens, whereas the putting surfaces at Quaker Ridge are set at grade level and designed to accommodate run-up shots. The resulting greens look fairly level, but appearances are deceiving. With the greens sitting on natural slopes rather than being artificially propped up, their contours blend seamlessly into the surrounding terrain and thus are hard to discern when viewed up close.

A succession of demanding par 4s—with their canted fairways—makes Quaker Ridge a relentless test of driving. The 429-yard seventh hole doglegs sharply to the right and demands a carefully controlled fade to avoid running through the fairway. From there, a long, uphill second shot is required to reach the most elevated green on the course.

The eighth hole, at 359 yards the layout's shortest par 4, features a pair of natural rock outcroppings at mid-fairway that Tillinghast turfed over and planted as rough. The roller-coaster fairway splits around them. An architect confronting such mounds today would surely try to blast them away. But classicists work with, rather than against, the land, and that's what makes Quaker Ridge so intriguing.

Recently, when Ben Crenshaw played a round here, he fell in love with the eighth fairway. Later, as he looked out upon the course from the German Tudor clubhouse, Crenshaw turned to his hosts and asked, "Can't you just hear Tillie with the mules and shapers working those mounds?"
—*Bradley S. Klein*

| Par | 70 |
| --- | --- |
| Yards | 6,849 |
| Slope | 143 |
| Rating | 73.9 |

**Golfweek Rating**
7.67

Classic *course profile*

**Architect:** Seth Raynor, 1921    **Superintendent:** Timothy F. Davis

# Shoreacres

## Lake Bluff, Illinois

Meandering around several ravines and large trees just off the coast of Lake Michigan, ultra-private Shoreacres is one of American golf's purest walks in the park. At times a golfer might feel he is traveling back in time, starting with the drive up the curving lane that doubles as a nature trail on the way to an understated white clubhouse.

One of Raynor's best layouts, Shoreacres is both unique and challenging. Don't let the yardage fool you. Though it stretches to all of 6,318 yards, the course is demanding as well as fun because of narrow, tree-lined fairways; large, undulating greens that are fast and guarded by angled bunkers; numerous deep ravines; and doglegs on which picking the right line is not always easy.

Old-style Shoreacres starts slowly but steadily builds speed with an onslaught of outstanding holes, both short and long. The par-3 Biarritz sixth, 190 yards, features an 83-yard-long green with a dip across the middle; depending on hole placement, a player could use any one of five or six clubs because of the green's depth. The par-3 12th is played from an elevated tee to a green in a shaded ravine. It is sandwiched between two terrific short par 4s—the 11th guarded by ravines right and in front of the green, and the dogleg-left 13th, where a blind tee shot is hit from ravine up to a fairway beyond a cliff.

The golf-only Shoreacres is the second or third club to many of its members. In fact, at least a couple of its members are said to violate the 14-club rule—meaning they belong to more than 14 private golf clubs.

*—Jeff Rude*

| | |
|---|---|
| **Par** | 71 |
| **Yards** | 6,318 |
| **Slope** | 135 |
| **Rating** | 71.1 |

***Golfweek* Rating**

7.56

**Architect:** Donald J. Ross, 1921    **Superintendent:** Gregory G. James

# Plainfield Country Club

## Plainfield, New Jersey

It's easy to overlook Plainfield; it sits in the kind of neighborhood you see at the beginning of *The Sopranos*. At 6,887 yards, it's not a power golf course. But that's because Donald Ross knew the one thing that never goes out of date is ground contour. On these greens, there's plenty of it.

You can get vertigo standing on some of these putting surfaces. The greens on the two short par 3s, the sixth (141 yards) and 11th (147), look like they are ready to slide down the hill. The ground slopes for some of the par 4s are just as interesting. None is more devilish than uphill fourth hole, a 331-yard reverse-camber hole with a fairway that defies gravity and a tiny little green perched just beyond deep bunkers.

Plainfield's finish is especially strong. The uphill par-5 16th brings a huge cross bunker into play on the second shot. The dogleg-right 17th requires a drive threaded into the corner. And the drive on the 384-yard 18th has to work gently the other way, right to left, to leave a decent angle into the green.

With shotmaking demands like that, it's no wonder Plainfield has held up well in its two majors, the 1978 U.S. Amateur (won by John Cook) and the 1987 U.S. Women's Open (Laura Davies). With the course just now coming out of a long-term restoration by Gil Hanse, there's every reason to believe it will continue to challenge golfers for decades to come.

—*Bradley S. Klein*

| | |
|---|---|
| **Par** | **72** |
| **Yards** | **6,887** |
| **Slope** | **136** |
| **Rating** | **73.6** |

***Golfweek* Rating**

**7.55**

*Architect:* A. W. Tillinghast, 1918    *Superintendent:* Robert Dwyer, CGCS

# Somerset Hills Country Club

## Bernardsville, New Jersey

Halfway through the front nine at Somerset Hills in central New Jersey, you realize something about the Golden Age architects. A. W. Tillinghast and his cohorts—Charles Blair Macdonald, Alister MacKenzie—were out there having fun as they worked, and they wanted other golfers to share in the joy and exhilaration of trying to play around or on top of these outlandish features they kept creating. They certainly weren't trying to appease golfers, and they also didn't worry about making friends with the public.

Nobody would build this stuff today—huge vaulted greens that cascade down from back to front; wild chocolate-drop mounds—"the Dolomites"—separating parallel holes and adjacent greens. The 11th hole flows down and away, banking right to left as it doglegs right to left. The hole is called "Perfection," but it feels more like "vertigo."

Late in his career, Tillinghast made a feeble Depression-era living removing bunkers from golf courses to spare clubs excess maintenance cost. Somehow, he removed nearly 100 from Somerset Hills, but that still left about 150, and most of them seem to be just where you want to hit the ball.

The front nine at this splendid old club has an open, farm field sensibility; the back nine is rockier, steeper and more densely wooded. Together, they conspire to create one of the great gems of classical architecture.

—*Bradley S. Klein*

| | |
|---|---|
| **Par** | 71 |
| **Yards** | 6,659 |
| **Slope** | 129 |
| **Rating** | 70.4 |

**Golfweek Rating**
7.53

***Architects:*** Donald Ross, 1924 • Robert Trent Jones Sr., 1955 • George & Tom Fazio, 1979
***Superintendent:*** Jeff Corcoran, CGCS

# Oak Hill Country Club *(East)*

## Pittsford, New York

| | |
|---|---|
| **Par** | 71 |
| **Yards** | 6,902 |
| **Slope** | 137 |
| **Rating** | 74.4 |

**Golfweek Rating**
**7.52**

Hard to believe the acreage that now is home to Oak Hill Country Club once was described as "barren, cheerless and singularly lacking in beauty." That's hardly an apt description of the place today. Oak Hill's East Course is the more famed of the club's two 18-hole layouts. It weaves through a breathtaking collection of majestic oaks, the result of quite possibly the mightiest tree-planting program in all of golf.

The golf course is demanding off the tee, and approach shots must be played to medium-sized greens with slight undulations. There are water hazards on five holes.

Oak Hill's most distinctive hole is the 594-yard 13th, which requires a well-struck tee shot down a narrow fairway and an approach shot that must be played to a well-guarded green. A creek bisects the hole at 300 yards and meanders down the fairway. Until today's generation of technology, no one ever anticipated the hole would be reached in two shots.

In addition to the 2003 PGA Championship, Oak Hill has played host to the U.S. Open in 1956, 1968 (Lee Trevino's first pro victory) and 1989, the PGA in 1980, the U.S. Amateur in 1949 and 1999, the U.S. Senior Open in 1985, and the Ryder Cup in 1995, when Nick Faldo got up-and-down for par at 18 from the fairway to cap a come-from-behind, 1-up victory over Curtis Strange. Strange had enjoyed earlier success at Oak Hill, capturing the Open in 1989.

It was at Oak Hill-East's 17th that Ben Hogan missed a 30-inch putt that kept him from a possible playoff for his fifth U.S. Open title in 1956.

"I guess I'm kind of glad I missed it," Hogan sighed afterward. "I'd hate to have to go out there again tomorrow."

*—Jeff Babineau*

**Architects:** Tom Bendelow, 1928 • Roger Packard, 1986    **Superintendent:** Thomas Lively, CGCS

# Medinah Country Club (No. 3)

## Medinah, Illinois

| Par | 72 |
|---|---|
| Yards | 7,401 |
| Slope | 149 |
| Rating | 77.1 |

***Golfweek* Rating**

**7.50**

Founded when a group of Shriners from Chicago's Medinah Temple decided to create a 54-hole country retreat, Medinah Country Club now encompasses 640 acres. The prime tract is the No. 3 course, a design by Scotland-born Tom Bendelow that has undergone numerous facelifts, the first only three years after it opened.

What hasn't changed much is the sense of forest. The No. 3 course features about 4,200 trees, more than 200 per hole, mainly red, white and burr oak and hickory. Little wonder, then, why Alistair Cooke, in his foreword to *The World Atlas of Golf*, described Medinah No. 3 as a "claustrophobia of woods." And little wonder why locals refer to the 3-iron as the Medinah club, for it is used often to punch out back to the fairway.

Medinah is all brute. There aren't many breathers. At the end of the narrow, tree-lined fairways are fast, undulating greens that average 6,200 square feet. Medinah No. 3 measured 7,401 yards when Tiger Woods won the 1999 PGA Championship. Six par 4s played at least 439 yards. The dogleg-left 16th, played to an elevated green, is among the most challenging par 4s in golf.

The short holes are no bargain, either. Nos. 2, 13 and 17 are par 3s over Lake Kadijah. The 17th green has been moved more than some of the skin on Cher's body. It was moved off the water before the 1999 PGA, but it's back on the lake as part of a Rees Jones makeover.

Medinah also has been host to three U.S. Opens—won by Cary Middlecoff in 1949, Lou Graham in 1975 and Hale Irwin in 1990. It also has hosted the 1988 U.S. Senior Open and three Western Opens. Next up are the 2006 PGA and the 2012 Ryder Cup.

*—Jeff Rude*

# Maidstone Club

## East Hampton, New York

Out on the south shore of easternmost Long Island, pure links conditions prevail. The wind howls off the Atlantic Ocean. Primary and secondary dune lines provide a perfect setting for golf holes. The salty sea air refreshes awareness of the elements.

Without good golf holes, such a setting is wasted—like a well-decorated restaurant that offers no fare. What makes golf at the Maidstone Club so compelling is that the land is well used and doesn't allow for a lull. The out-and-back routing meanders around 88-acre Hook Pond on its way to the ocean's edge. There, two short par 3s, the eighth and 14th, sit in the middle of the dunes and serve as culmination points for the round.

The longer holes also are beautifully shaped, with fairway turns difficult to negotiate once the wind takes hold or the ball simply rolls out on the fast turf. It makes for a game measured not in yardages but in ability to control the shot.

—*Bradley S. Klein*

| | |
|---|---|
| **Par** | 72 |
| **Yards** | 6,403 |
| **Slope** | 136 |
| **Rating** | 71.9 |

**Golfweek Rating**

7.50

Classic course profile

Architect: A. W. Tillinghast, 1923    Superintendent: Joseph Eric Greytok

# Winged Foot Golf Club (East)

## Mamaroneck, New York

| | |
|---|---|
| Par | 72 |
| Yards | 6,664 |
| Slope | 135 |
| Rating | 72.2 |

**Golfweek Rating**

**7.50**

When a course is rated among *Golfweek*'s top layouts in the country, rarely can it be said that it's only the second best track on the property.

Such is the case with Winged Foot East, which is ranked 18 spots behind its sister course, the West. But if you go to Winged Foot and play the East, you'll know it's more than just a consolation prize.

The Winged Foot courses are said to be among A. W. Tillinghast's crowning achievements in golf, and this in a portfolio that includes Baltusrol, Bethpage, Quaker Ridge and Ridgewood. The East and West are the only "twin" courses on *Golfweek*'s top 50 list of Classical courses. Winged Foot joins Bandon Dunes Resort (Modern list) as the only properties with two courses in the top 50 on either list.

The East is a slightly shorter, softer test, yet still presents a challenge because it also is a bit tighter. The East course shares many of the West's characteristics, including flashed-up bunkers and elevated greens—where Tillinghast liked to pay particular attention. "Golf holes are like men," he said, "all rather similar from foot to neck, with the greens showing the same varying characteristics as human faces."

Winged Foot's East Course has been the site of three USGA championships, including the inaugural U.S. Senior Open in 1980 (won by Roberto De Vicenzo) and two U.S. Women's Opens (Betsy Rawls won in 1957 and Susie Maxwell Berning triumphed in 1972). During the '57 Women's Open, the course was the scene of a heartbreaking incident that saw Jackie Pung disqualified after she signed an incorrect scorecard for what should have been a winning score, thereby handing the championship to Rawls.

—*Jeff Barr*

# Pinehurst
## The Premier Open Layout

### By James Achenbach

Bethpage Black is a fabulous U.S. Open course, but it isn't the best. From where I sit, that honor goes to Pinehurst No. 2.

What are the 10 best U.S. Open courses? Tiger Woods might start with Pebble Beach and Bethpage, where he has won his two U.S. Opens. However, because I haven't won the U.S. Open, I am without prejudice (I also am without a golf game, but that's another story).

### *James Achenbach's U.S. Open Top 10*

### 1. Pinehurst (No. 2)

This extraordinarily playable resort facility (it is almost impossible to lose a ball here) played host to its first U.S. Open in 1999 and quickly earned a return ticket for 2005. It richly deserved such an honor. With a collection of roly-poly Donald Ross greens and a multitude of chipping areas, No. 2 placed a premium on iron play and recovery shots. The course didn't even require the barbed-wire rough that is grown for most Opens (including Bethpage). The 1999 event was more fun to watch than any other recent U.S. Open.

### 2. Pebble Beach

The crown jewel of the U.S. Open rotation, Pebble is loved by everyone. This is the most scenic Open site. Forget the opening holes—they are merely an appetizer. The sixth through the 10th have become America's most famous stretch of holes, surpassing even the 11th, 12th and 13th at Augusta National.

### 3. Shinnecock Hills

Golfers can thank former USGA president Harry Easterly for bringing the Open back to Shinnecock. The championship was held there in 1896, and then didn't return until 90 years later in 1986. Located near the eastern end of Long Island, Shinnecock is more like a British Open layout than any other U.S. Open course. This is the ultimate challenge for all-around shotmaking and mental tenacity.

### 4. Bethpage (Black)

A sprawling, visually stunning layout, Bethpage seemed instantaneously comfortable in playing host to this championship for the first time. The players loved it, the fans loved it, and Bethpage is here to stay.

### 5. Olympic (Lake)

Famous as the place where two golf legends lost Open playoffs—Ben Hogan to Jack Fleck in 1955 and Arnold Palmer to Billy Casper in 1966—Olympic is a glamorous Open site because of its San Francisco location. More than this, however, it offers the best U.S. Open examination of driving the ball.

### 6. Baltusrol (Lower)

You have to love a course that has no par 5s among the first 16 holes. Both 17 and 18 are par 5s, but most players have been hammered long before then. Accuracy and course management are the keys here.

### 7. Oakmont
Boasts the most interesting greens of all the Open courses.

### 8. Winged Foot (West)
When the U.S. Open returns here in 2006 after a 22-year absence, the setup will be the key. It was dubbed the "Massacre at Winged Foot" when Hale Irwin won with a 7-over-par total in 1974, yet Fuzzy Zoeller was 11 shots lower when he won in 1984.

### 9. Oakland Hills (South)
Hogan won here, but so did Andy North and Steve Jones, making Oakland Hills perhaps the most mysterious Open course.

### 10. Merion (East)
Sadly, Merion may never host another Open. The course seems too short, the size and location too cramped for the Open infrastructure.

The 2002 Open at Bethpage was nicknamed the "People's Open," and what a great U.S. Open it was.

To demonstrate its commitment to public golf, the USGA quickly announced that the 2009 Open will be at Bethpage Black, a public facility that is owned and operated by the state of New York and a place where a golfer can play for $31 during the week and $39 on weekends.

There is a modern precedent for announcing a quick return to a U.S. Open site. A year after it served as host for the 1999 Open, Pinehurst No. 2 was chosen for 2005. In a marvelous coupling of public golf—one on the east coast and the other on the west coast—Torrey Pines in LaJolla, California, will play host to the 2008 Open and join Bethpage Black in the affordable category.

Private courses own Open history, so it's no wonder that the 2013 Open apparently will be played at The Country Club in Brookline, Massachusetts. This will mark the 100-year anniversary of the stunning Open victory by amateur Francis Ouimet at the same course.

The U.S. Open is heading into a new era in which private, resort and public courses are united in a commendable trifecta.

**Payne Stewart clinches the 1999 U.S. Open at Pinehurst (No. 2).** *Tom Able-Green/Getty Images*

Domed greens, like at the par-3 6th hole, make for difficult approach shots at Pinehurst (No. 2).

**Architects:** Donald J. Ross, 1919 • George & Tom Fazio, 1978    **Superintendent:** Thomas F. Walker

# Inverness Club

## Toledo, Ohio

Few golf courses combine history and challenge the way Inverness does. Here's a layout that has vexed the world's finest players since the 1920 U.S. Open, when Englishman Ted Ray squeaked by his compatriot, Harry Vardon. That was the first major event to welcome golf professionals into the clubhouse. The grateful pros took up a collection for a chime clock that stands today in the clubhouse lobby and carries an inscription:

*God measures men by what they are*
*Not what in wealth they possess*
*This vibrant message chimes afar*
*The voice of Inverness*

The 1931 U.S. Open at Inverness took a 72-hole playoff before Billy Burke beat George Von Elm by a single stroke. In 1957, little-known Dick Mayer needed an 18-hole playoff to defeat one of the game's dominant players of the time, Cary Middlecoff. In 1979, Hale Irwin won the U.S. Open at Inverness, but the most memorable moment of that event followed tour pro Lon Hinkle's first-round play down the 17th fairway as a shortcut to the par-5 8th hole. The USGA took the unprecedented step of planting a Black Hills spruce tree overnight to thwart subsequent shortcuts. More than two decades later, when Inverness officials undertook an extensive tree management plan to deal with surplus trees, the ungainly spruce survived the cuts. History proved more important than aesthetics.

Inverness combines length, shotmaking and tiny, well-contoured greens. Its most famous hole, the 354-yard par-4 18th, is also one of the shortest finishing holes in championship golf. It was here in 1986 that Bob Tway holed out from a greenside bunker to defeat Greg Norman by a shot in the 1986 PGA championship.

—*Bradley S. Klein*

| Par | 71 |
|---|---|
| Yards | 7,255 |
| Slope | 144 |
| Rating | 75.9 |

**Golfweek Rating**
**7.49**

# Baltimore Country Club *(East)*

## Timonium, Maryland

Baltimore Country Club's East Course has impeccable design credentials and an even more impressive tournament history. The club's in-town course played host to the 1899 U.S. Open. A. W. Tillinghast designed and built the current layout on a site west of town called Five Farms.

The rolling terrain was partially treed, but there also was enough clear ground for Tillinghast to create an unusually diverse set of holes. As he wrote of Five Farms in 1932, "as is usual with my courses, there are no mighty carries necessary from the tee and the fairways are comparatively open, but the contours of the greens make careful placements necessary to getting home. It may be remarked here that the greens generally call for lofted approaches."

The course also played host to the 1928 PGA Championship (won by Leo Diegel), the 1932 U.S. Amateur (Sandy Somerville), the 1965 Walker Cup (the U.S. and GB&I tied) and the 1988 U.S. Women's Open (Liselotte Neumann).

None of the par 3s exceeds 180 yards, and all present small, well-sloped targets that fall off steeply on the sides and behind. The par 5s also are noteworthy, with the 584-yard sixth called "Barn" out of respect for the wooden red building, part of the old farm-style maintenance area that sits on the inside of the dogleg left. At the 603-yard 14th, named "Hell's Half Acre" (after the seventh hole at Pine Valley), Tillinghast reprises one of his favorite motifs, a massive mid-fairway bunker complex that must be carried on the second shot as the hole turns left. Similar hazards can be found at his Quaker Ridge 14th, Baltusrol (Lower) 17th, Baltusrol (Upper) 11th and Somerset Hills ninth.

—*Bradley S. Klein*

|  |  |
|---|---|
| **Par** | 70 |
| **Yards** | 6,681 |
| **Slope** | 132 |
| **Rating** | 72.6 |

***Golfweek* Rating**

7.48

**Classic** *course profile*

**Architects:** Robert Trent Jones Sr. & Robert Tyre "Bobby" Jones, 1948    **Superintendent:** William Shirley, CGCS

# Peachtree Golf Club

## Atlanta, Georgia

Peachtree is one of the country's landmark courses. Opened in 1948 and designed by two of the game's most famous personalities, it set the tone for the entire post-World War II era of course architecture. It was big and bold and called for a strong aerial game, often to greens perched up and protected by steep bunkers. And yet not only was Peachtree a trendsetter in its day, it continues to remain fresh and challenging, long after many courses that sought to emulate it have been bypassed as obsolete.

The site helped—250 acres, with big, broad elevation changes (85 feet from high point to low) that could be incorporated into quality holes. Peachtree was built before massive earth moving had become fashionable, and so the routing that the two Joneses arrived at had to be ideal. It was, with many holes calling for tees, fairway landing areas and green sites on natural rises, with the steepest ground arrayed in between or diagonally that golfers could hopscotch over them. Even then, they were also thinking about the future; there was plenty of ground left behind the back tees for lengthening, if needed. Today, Peachtree could still be stretched 300 yards without compromising the shotmaking or design intent.

Everywhere, the design influence of Augusta National is evident, from the minimal bunkering—only 50 on Peachtree, including only two holes with fairway bunkering that influences tee shots. Tees are big, the fairways are wide, and the Penncross bentgrass greens are large enough (7,000 square feet) so that even at modern speeds there are adequate hole locations and enough ground for the ball to come to rest.

Club officials know they have a gem that needs occasional refinement, whether for major competitions (like the 1989 Walker Cup) or for everyday member play. The beauty of a place like Peachtree—and there aren't many like it—is timeless. The course demonstrates the ongoing relevance of a distinct era in American golf architecture.

—*Bradley S. Klein*

| Par | 72 |
|---|---|
| **Yards** | **7,043** |
| **Slope** | **140** |
| **Rating** | **74.6** |

**Golfweek Rating**

**7.47**

© Tony Roberts

**Architect:** A. W. Tillinghast, 1922    **Superintendent:** Mark Hughes, CGCS

# Baltusrol Country Club (Lower)

## Springfield, New Jersey

Baltusrol's Lower is well known for its difficult and somewhat unusual finish of consecutive par 5s. The 630-yard 17th is one of America's truly great three-shot par 5s. During the 1993 U.S. Open, it took a monstrous drive and 295-yard 1-iron from John Daly, golf's version of Paul Bunyan, to make history by reaching the putting surface at 17.

But the Lower is not all about brawn. It also is famous for its par-3 fourth hole, guarded front and left by water. Robert Trent Jones Sr. made the original par 3 more severe to add a little muscle to the course for the 1954 U.S. Open. In response to criticism that he had made the fourth too tough, Jones invited his critics to join him on the fourth tee, where Jones took out a 5-iron and launched a shot that ended up in the cup for an ace. "Gentlemen, as you can see," he said, "the hole is eminently fair."

Baltusrol's Lower made its championship debut by playing host to the 1926 U.S. Amateur (where Bobby Jones was defeated by George Von Elm). It subsequently held the U.S. Open in 1936, 1946, 1954, 1967 and 1980.

That later Open saw Jack Nicklaus and Isao Aoki stage an epic duel that Nicklaus eventually won. In 1993, Lee Janzen won his first U.S. Open. The Lower hosted the U.S. Women's Open in 1961, where the great Mickey Wright prevailed.

—*Jeff Babineau*

| | |
|---|---|
| **Par** | 72 |
| **Yards** | 7,221 |
| **Slope** | 139 |
| **Rating** | 75.5 |

**Golfweek Rating**

7.44

**Architect:** William S. Flynn, 1923    **Superintendent:** Douglas A. Miller, CGCS

# Cascades Golf Club

## Hot Springs, Virginia

Mountain golf courses are notoriously hard to do well. The land usually overwhelms the site. Yet Cascades Golf Club at The Homestead Resort works surprisingly well despite 150 feet of natural elevation change across occasionally rough terrain in the Allegheny Range, 1,150 feet above sea level.

Working in 1923, when earth-moving capabilities and budgets were sorely limited, architect William S. Flynn used his considerable routing skills on what amounts to a narrow defile of golf course. The holes go out and back in links style and make fine use of the Cascades Stream as it meanders across the site.

Cascades incorporates long, dramatic downhill tee shots with the occasional tough uphill shot, as at the short par-4 third, the stutter-step par-5 fifth, and the approach into the par-4 seventh green. The course ends on a relatively broad, lower-lying expanse, with an unusual concluding sequence of pars 3-5-5-3.

Cascades has long been a favorite stopping point for USGA championships, including the 1928 U.S. Women's Amateur, the 1966 Curtis Cup, the 1967 U.S. Women's Open, the 1980 USGA Senior Amateur, the 1988 U.S. Amateur, and the 2000 U.S. Mid-Amateur.

*—Bradley S. Klein*

| | |
|---|---|
| **Par** | **70** |
| **Yards** | **6,679** |
| **Slope** | **137** |
| **Rating** | **73.0** |

***Golfweek* Rating**
**7.44**

# Architects
## *Obstacles, Not Length, Needed*

**By James Achenbach**

Modern golf balls and clubs are causing a headache for golf course designers, and the antidote is not a double dose of aspirin. The common remedy, albeit temporary, is to heap more yardage onto what already is a perceptible movement toward 8,000-yard courses.

Architect Steve Smyers is constructing a par-70 course, Charter Oak Golf Club, in Goshen, Connecticut, that measures 7,400 yards from the back tees. "You have to do it," he said.

Pete Dye, surveying his new Country Club of the Desert course in La Quinta, California, once again screeched his dissent.

"This is terrible," Dye said of today's longer courses. "On every hole, I have to build a tee so far back there that it seems like it's on the other side of town. I think all that yardage they added at Augusta National is the worst thing that could have happened to golf. The sport has gone crazy. People aren't honest about what is happening."

And what is happening?

"All these advances in equipment are helping the best players make a joke of the game. These balls help the tour players enormously, but they don't help the rest of us as much. It should be the other way around. There should be balls that are helping us but not them."

Then Dye launched into his famous monologue about the need for a shorter ball for touring pros. He has said many times that the Masters, being an invitational, should introduce a decompressed tournament ball and force all the players to use it.

Most research supports Dye's theory about golf balls. Golfers able to hit the ball extremely high without much backspin ("high launch, low spin") are gaining significant extra yardage from today's solid-core, multicover golf balls.

As a result, yardage barriers constantly are being expanded and courses must be updated. Said Smyers of his celebrated Old Memorial course in Tampa: "We designed it in 1994, and the thing now is so antiquated [by pro standards] it's incredible."

Architect Bobby Weed, looking into his crystal ball, sees a monster—the 400-yard drive. "There are a busload of kids out there who hit it forever, and 300-yard drives are commonplace today," Weed said. "We are coming up on 400-yard drives. They are right around the corner."

And what is being done about this?

The U.S. Golf Association is attempting to put the brakes on increased yardage. The USGA is trying to update the Overall Distance Standard and stop golf ball scientists from leapfrogging the rules. The ODS was adopted in 1976, but this hasn't stopped ball makers from using new materials, new designs and new aerodynamic patterns to produce golf balls that seem supercharged when hit by the most skilled players.

Designer Keith Foster, who renovated Southern Hills Country Club in Tulsa before the 2001 U.S. Open, says bluntly that many

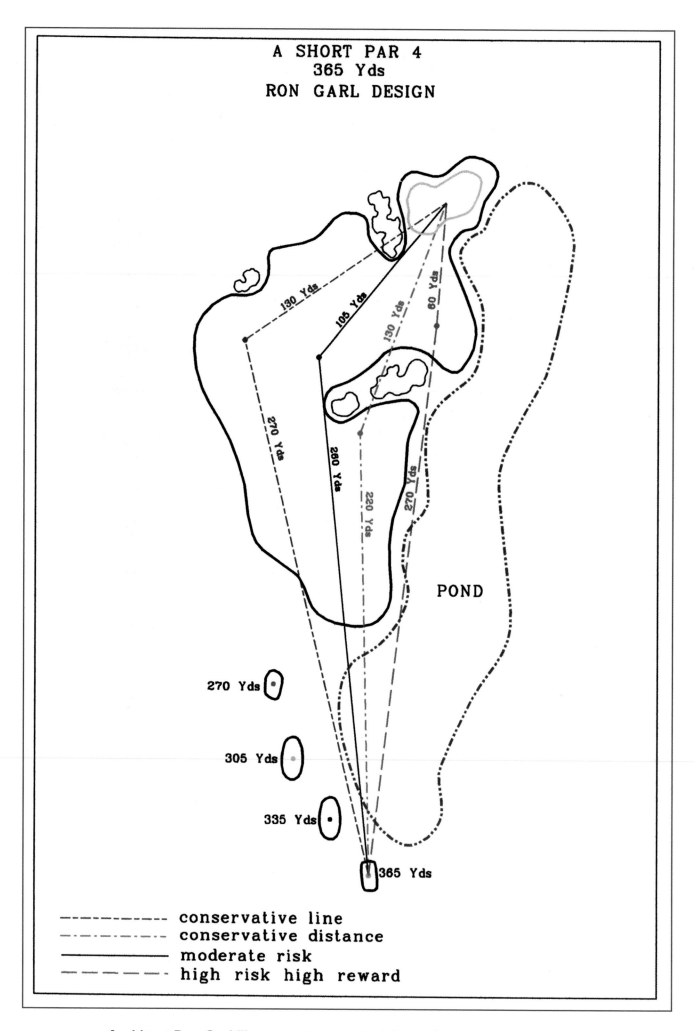

# A SHORT PAR 4
## 365 Yds
### RON GARL DESIGN

POND

270 Yds

305 Yds

335 Yds

365 Yds

130 Yds
105 Yds
130 Yds
60 Yds
270 Yds
260 Yds
220 Yds
270 Yds

- - - - - - - - - - - conservative line
- · - · - · - · - · - conservative distance
――――――――― moderate risk
- - - - - - - - - high risk high reward

**Architect Ron Garl illustrates hypothetical lines of play on a short par 4.**

of the old courses are unsuitable as a test for today's players.

"I remember when I started my career with Art Hills," Foster said, "and the turn point [for doglegs] was 250 yards. Then it became 260. Then it became 270."

The result, according to Foster, is that architects are obligated to leave room for future expansion.

"If technology continues to go nuts, the back tees will be pushed back, back, back." he said. The problem, of course, is that we also need more land. Bigger golf courses require more length and more width."

Architect Ron Garl focuses on one obvious solution—that landing areas for longer hitters need to get narrower—as well as some other approaches.

"How about a combination of crossing bunkers, tree placements and different hazards where the reward truly equals the risk?" Garl asks. "We have to throw up some obstacles, or the game will be ruined. Look at the 13th at Augusta National. The creek hardly comes into play any more."

Garl's solution, on a hole such as the 13th, is to "force them to hit a shorter shot off the tee. Then they've got the same distance into the green that Ben Hogan had. They may not hit the same club, but they've got the same shot with the same length and the same objective, which is to get it close and make the putt."

Smyers sees more par-70 courses in the future. Foster sees a greater range on par 3s and par 4s.

"It wouldn't surprise me to see 240- and 250-yard par 3s on many of the new courses," Foster said. "I am doing this right now. At the same time, let me say that the golf courses I find most interesting are not the 7,300- and 7,400-yard courses. I like the quirky courses, the shotmaking courses."

Foster and many other designers have a great admiration for the short par 4.

"My favorite hole is the short par 4," Garl said. "We need to be creative and continue to build them. So what if occasionally we take the driver out of the hands of the longest players? Golf is meant to be an all-around challenge. It's not just a driving game."

Realistically, bunkers must be moved.

"Moving the bunkers, moving the angle turns," Weed said. "That's a response to the modern game. We've gone from Donald Ross in the 1940s at 600-feet angle turns to 900-feet angle turns now. Who's to say that won't continue?"

Smyers wants to penalize golfers if they can't work the ball.

"Nobody pays any attention to how easy it is to hit the golf ball straight compared with 20 years ago," he said. "It's going dead straight. So we should set up a hole where we encourage the player to work it into the wind. If he can't shape it, he loses it and he pays a penalty."

Foster advocates smaller greens and deeper bunkers, although he agrees with Weed about another growing danger.

"The gap is widening. There are more bad golfers than ever before," Weed said. "The basement stays the same, but the ceiling just keeps getting higher. We have never experienced a time when the gap is so wide."

And how do architects combat it?

"Rethink our angle turns, our bunkering, our strategic design," Weed said. "There is not enough emphasis on the mental side of the game, and all of us are looking for new ways to challenge the best players today.

And his final answer?

"It all goes back to the green complexes," Weed said. "There's still room for the illusions we use as architects, the tricks we rely on, the way we can affect depth perception—not having backdrops to the greens, having some greens that fall off, building false fronts, letting some greens fall away. All that makes the golfer think more. Touring pros get so accustomed to flying the ball to the hole. We have to be willing to challenge them."

**Architect:** Donald J. Ross, 1912 & 1915   **Superintendent:** John Steiner, CGCS

# White Bear Yacht Club

## White Bear Lake, Minnesota

*Classic course profile*

| Par | 72 |
|---|---|
| Yards | 6,471 |
| Slope | 137 |
| Rating | 72.5 |

**Golfweek Rating**

**7.43**

White Bear Yacht Club is one of the purest remaining versions of Donald Ross' early design work. The routing has scarcely changed since Ross completed work there in 1915. The club, on the far northeast side of St. Paul, occupies a dramatically rolling site and straddles Stillwater Road, with each nine incorporating a hole where the drive plays across the two-lane street.

Ross, working without earth-moving equipment in those days, kept his bunkers low. The bulk of them were placed in the run-up areas and in front of greens, as well as along the deep side of the fairway landing ones. In this manner, Ross followed a basic design principle that guided his routings—build holes that play over deep swales so that the golf takes place from high point to high point.

At the 552-yard, par-5 fourth hole, the tee shot calls for a carry across an extended hollow. The maintenance crew has completed a rebuilding of the wood bridge from tee to fairway—20 feet high, 420 feet long. Its gnarly, weather-beaten character fits in perfectly with the rest of the place.

—*Bradley S. Klein*

**Architect:** Seth Raynor, 1925     **Superintendent:** James E. Yonce III

# Yeamans Hall Club

## Hanahan, South Carolina

There aren't many more intriguing entrances to a private club in America than this one. Once you cross the railroad tracks, you leave behind a blighted commercial zone and enter a cultural Time Tunnel. You pass vast lawns with huge live oaks and behind them, elegant wooden houses. The unpaved road ambles across what you later find out is the first fairway and leads to a collection of simple plantation-style buildings that serve as clubhouse, pro shop and guest quarters. That's when it hits you. This is what the South used to be like.

Yeamans Hall is one of Seth Raynor's finest designs. The holes weave their way around a marshy lowlands site and bring those gracious old homes into view without ever playing up to them. And as you walk around the course you simply marvel at how Raynor brought all of his familiar holes with him and managed to make them work despite an absence of elevation change.

He dug a little, piled some dirt, and between the low-lying bunker floor and the slightly elevated green surface, created all the vertical drama he needed.

Among the many students of architecture fascinated by Yeamans' raw, bony features is longtime superintendent Jim Yonce. His home on site serves as a virtual library for researching the architecture. What a coincidence. The 18 holes in his back yard provide the same service.

—*Bradley S. Klein*

| Par | 70 |
|---|---|
| Yards | 6,679 |
| Slope | 132 |
| Rating | 72.3 |

**Golfweek Rating**
**7.43**

**Architect:** Donald J. Ross, 1925    **Superintendent:** Kip Tyler, CGCS

# Salem Country Club

## Peabody, Massachusetts

Salem Country Club is rich in history. The club's logo—the silhouette of a witch flying on a broom—evokes distant events that made famous the nearby town of Salem. More recently, the club has created much local lore, thanks to five USGA championships held on its Ross-designed fairways: the 1932 U.S. Women's Amateur (won by Virginia Van Wie); the 1954 U.S. Women's Open (Babe Didrikson Zaharias); the 1977 USGA Senior Amateur (Dale Morey); the 1984 U.S. Women's Open (Hollis Stacy); and the 2001 U.S. Senior Open (Bruce Fleisher).

Here is a classic New England parkland layout, with tree-lined fairways and wide corridors of play that fill a rolling, 250-acre former farm site. Exposed ledge and rock walls are scattered throughout the ground. The kick and bite of Ross' original green contours are very much in evidence, making for very precise iron play to bentgrass/poa annua greens where position is nearly everything if there is any hope to get down in two putts.

One way to beat these devilish slopes is do what Hollis Stacy did on Salem's famed 13th hole in the fourth round of the 1984 Women's Open (for major play, the nines are reversed from normal member play). From down in the right rough inside the dogleg, she scraped out a 7-iron that scooted up to the green and into the hole for eagle. The miracle recovery vaulted her into the lead, and she held on for a one-shot victory.

—*Bradley S. Klein*

| | |
|---|---|
| Par | 72 |
| Yards | 6,837 |
| Slope | 144 |
| Rating | 72 |

**Golfweek** Rating

7.42

# Myopia Hunt Club

## Hamilton, Massachusetts

Myopia Hunt is no mere museum piece. Though it opened in an era of hickory shafts and gutta-percha golf balls, it continues to instruct and bedevil players who think the modern game is qualitatively different than classical golf.

It was good enough to host four of the first 14 U.S. Opens (1898, 1901, 1905 and 1908). Though only 6,539 yards from the back tee, it also proved tough enough during the 2003 Massachusetts Mid-Amateur that only six of the 270 rounds played during the championship produced under-par scores. At a total of 2 under par for the three-round event, Frank Vana Jr., won by a whopping six strokes.

Myopia Hunt sits on a mere 120 acres and has scarcely changed since its U.S. Open days. The greens have been squared off and recaptured somewhat in size, the bunkers deepened and a few holes lengthened marginally. The basic character still derives from uneven ground, lots of mounds, knee-high native fescue and bluestem roughs, and firm, fast and well-bunkered greens that average only 4,800 square feet in size.

Often, there's not a lot to look at off the tee, which can have an intimidating effect. Other times, what you're seeing at Myopia Hunt simply defies belief. Consider the club's most famous hole, the 136-yard, par-3 9th. The green here, surrounded by deep bunkers, is only 2,100 square feet large (small) and measures exactly 19 feet in width. There's nothing to hit to and even less to miss. Old-fashioned golf like this wasn't politically correct enough to worry about being fair. The beauty about golf at Myopia Hunt is that no matter how far you hit the ball in the air, the trouble begins when the ball hits the ground.

—*Bradley S. Klein*

| | |
|---|---|
| **Par** | 72 |
| **Yards** | 6,539 |
| **Slope** | 128 |
| **Rating** | 72 |

***Golfweek* Rating**
**7.42**

# East Lake Golf Club

## Atlanta, Georgia

### The Heart and Soul of a New Atlanta

*By Bradley S. Klein*

Occasionally, a well-executed restoration effort can spark an entirely new interest in the golf course. In the case of East Lake Golf Club, that renewal extended to include the entire neighborhood.

The course dates to 1908, when the Atlanta Athletic Club built a Tom Bendelow-designed layout on wooded parkland at the end point of an electric streetcar line that ran downtown. Donald Ross rerouted the course in 1915, and in 1925 he returned to add a second course. In those days, reliable Bermuda-grass greens were a shaky undertaking, which is why Ross created double greens for each hole, one for summer play and one for use during winter months. The consolidation of these into unified greens only took place long after Ross left the grounds. To further complete the genealogy of the golf course, George Cobb performed a "modernization" of the main 18-hole layout in 1959 in preparation for the 1963 Ryder Cup matches. Not until 1994, however, following a masterful reconstruction of the championship course by Rees Jones, did the layout achieve real grandeur.

The course always enjoyed a glorious history, in large measure because it was the home course of Bobby Jones. It also had a distinguished membership that made extensive use of the 36-hole layout and its vast, Tudor-style clubhouse. Gradually, however, the club's fortunes waned, in large part owing to the deterioration of the surrounding neighborhood. The AAC's two courses remained busy, but use of the club's dining and other social facilities slowed down as members feared venturing through the area's streets to reach the club. In an emotionally contentious decision in 1966, the

| Par | 72 |
|-----|-----|
| **Yards** | 7,207 |
| **Slope** | 139 |
| **Rating** | 74.9 |

**Golfweek Rating**

**7.36**

AAC sold off the second golf course and moved to a 600-acre site in Duluth, a northeast suburb of Atlanta.

The remaining course became part of a newly formed East Lake Golf Club. Across the street, on the land where the second layout once stood, sprawled an ill-conceived housing project that further contributed to the area's decline.

Businessman Tom Cousins came along in 1993 and set out to salvage East Lake. Under the aegis of the East Lake Community Foundation, Cousins proposed a public-private partnership to rehabilitate the golf course and the surrounding community. He then hired Rees Jones as his golf course architect.

Whatever charm the older incarnations of the course might have had, the new version is simply stunning. Strictly speaking, this was not a pure restoration, because there was no chance of going back to Ross' double greens. There weren't any detailed Ross maps or blueprints to go by, either—only old aerial and ground photography. This meant that Jones had to make crucial decisions about repositioning greens and adding contours. Along the way, he stripped the course, reworked the slopes, reconstructed every bunker, put in new irrigation and drainage, and regrassed the entire layout—meyer zoysia-grass fairways; crenshaw bentgrass greens; 419 Bermuda grass for the rough. The only significant routing tweak was swinging the old 17th fairway and green to the left so that they now sit astride the shore of 27-acre East Lake.

The result has been an impressive revival, not only of the golf course but also of the club and surrounding community. The clubhouse has been fully restored, an extensive caddie program provides employment opportunity for dozens of local youth, and a new second golf course has an extensive junior golf program for area residents. The main course hasn't done badly either, having hosted the PGA Tour's season-ending Tour Championship in 1998, 2000 and 2002 as well as the U.S. Amateur in 2001.

## America's Best: Rater's Notebook

### 1. Ease and intimacy of routing: 8
An old-fashioned routing, set up in linear fashion. The holes sit either parallel or at right angles to one another to conform to the large symmetrical rectangular site that has a clubhouse right in the middle.

### 2. Integrity of original design: 7
Has the look and feel of a 1920s movie that has been colorized, facelifted and smoothed over, with some of quirkiness lost in the process.

### 3. Natural setting and overall land plan: 5
You really feel in an old-fashioned semi-urbanized enclave, with modest houses rimming the place on the other side of the fence, looking in. The lack of interesting external views forces your attention inward.

### 4. Interest of greens and surrounding contours: 7
Greens look relatively level, but that's deceptive because they sit on ground that has more native contour than readily can be spotted.

### 5. Variety and memorability of par 3s: 9
A real strong suit, what with one of the country's oldest peninsula greens (sixth hole), a deceptive 11th that allows for run-up shots, plus a long, scary, slightly uphill 18th that makes East Lake the highest-rated course in the country to end on a par 3.

### 6. Variety and memorability of par 4s: 6
The eighth hole offers a fascinating array of fairway bunkers and mounds, some of them derived from old Civil War entrenchments. One factor that may soften the feel and impact of these holes is the low-profile bunkering and the gentle, rolled-down faces of the hazards.

### 7. Variety and memorability of par 5s: 7
All four par 5s play from east to west, but on different enough terrain. Good second-shot options on the ninth. Most interesting strategically is the relatively short, uphill 15th, with a well-protected green set on a left-to-right axis.

### 8. Basic quality of conditioning: 8
Solid, dense turf cover, despite notoriously tough-to-manage Atlanta climate, where the weather is too hot and humid in the summer and too cold in the winter.

### 9. Landscape and tree management: 8
Tree-lined corridors have been kept playable and wide enough, and there are no frivolous ornamental plantings.

### 10. "Walk in the park" test: 9
The overall experience and ambiance of the place actually outshines the quality of the golf holes to make a round here a special event if the opportunity arises.

**Overall vote by *Golfweek* course raters: 7.36**

| Hole | 1 | 2 | 3 | 4 | 5 | 6 | 7 | 8 | 9 | Out | Card of the Course |
|------|---|---|---|---|---|---|---|---|---|-----|--------------------|
| Yardage | 424 | 195 | 387 | 440 | 561 | 163 | 394 | 405 | 584 | 3,553 | |
| Par | 4 | 3 | 4 | 4 | 5 | 3 | 4 | 4 | 5 | 36 | |

| Hole | 10 | 11 | 12 | 13 | 14 | 15 | 16 | 17 | 18 | In | Total |
|------|----|----|----|----|----|----|----|----|----|-----|-------|
| Yardage | 516 | 197 | 391 | 439 | 442 | 495 | 481 | 453 | 235 | 3,649 | 7,202 |
| Par | 5 | 3 | 4 | 4 | 4 | 5 | 4 | 4 | 3 | 36 | 72 |

*Architect:* Donald J. Ross, 1927    *Superintendent:* Ryan Blair

# Holston Hills Country Club

## Knoxville, Tennessee

The value of restoration never has been clearer than at Holston Hills Country Club. In recent years, a steady commitment to reclaiming lost putting surfaces, removing tree clutter, claiming avenues of play and rebuilding bunkers has yielded impressive results.

The course has a strong tournament history, including two NCAA Championships, eight Tennessee State Amateurs and the 2004 U.S. Women's Mid-Amateur Championship.

Keeping a 75-year-old Ross course relevant for modern play is no easy task. Credit goes to superintendent Ryan Blair, the consulting input of Tom Doak, and a membership willing to recognize that intriguing architecture can never be taken for granted.

The course sits on a gently rolling 160-acre site with 25 feet of natural elevation change and borders the Holston River. The Bermuda-grass fairways are 45-50 yards wide and stutter-step around cross bunkers, mounds and swales. The 475-yard par-5 seventh offers a two-tier landing area with diagonal bunkering in the second-shot landing area that forces a decision about going for the green in two or not. Stark, 15-foot high mounds sit in the middle of the landing area on the 380-yard, par-4 15th. The short, uphill par-4 16th, only 304 yards, offers deep trouble all the way down the right side and a postage stamp-sized green that rejects more shots than it accepts.

—*Bradley S. Klein*

| Par | 72 |
| Yards | 6,932 |
| Slope | 134 |
| Rating | 74.3 |

*Golfweek* Rating
7.33

# Give 'Em 10 Clubs, and See Where They Fall

### By Dave Seanor

Are you worried about the future of golf? Do you toss and turn at night, fretting over the scoring resistance of Augusta National?

Here's a solution: Implement a 10-club rule for championship play. Give players the option, allowing them to lift any four clubs before each round. Lob wedge, 9-iron, 3-iron, 3-wood on Thursday; LW, 5-iron, 3-iron, driver on Saturday.

other proposals to "protect the integrity" of classic courses, something's going to change—whether you like it or not.

Not that I believe there's a problem. The number of players who pose any threat to the integrity of the game is a microscopic fraction of the golf universe. Those who do are playing on the PGA Tour, which has no interest in changing its slogan to "These guys used to be good, before we changed the rules."

## "Something's going to change—whether you like it or not."

During visits to the practice range at Bay Hill and The Players Championship, I first floated the idea of an 11- or 12-club limit and asked if it would affect scoring.

"What a stupid question," Steve Elkington scoffed.

"You're barking up the wrong tree, bro," said Vijay Singh. "The rule states 14 clubs. It will never change."

Not so fast, fellas. Never say never. With all the talk about deadening the golf ball and

But, hey, I'm not in charge. The U.S. Golf Association and Royal & Ancient call the shots, and they believe the game's under siege.

Everyone agrees that repelling the assault by lengthening courses is cost- and space-prohibitive. As for the so-called tournament ball, there's not enough room in this book to discuss the legal challenges that would ensue. And of course, nobody can stop athletes from growing larger, training more rigorously and seeking ever more sophisticated instruction.

"The 14-club limit was imposed because golf's ruling bodies feared the game was becoming too easy."

One answer is to challenge world-class players with narrower fairways, higher rough, deeper bunkers, firmer greens and tougher hole locations. The USGA and R&A have done that in their open championships, but at the risk of crossing the line of fairness.

So how about challenging them by reducing the number of clubs in their arsenal?

There is precedent. The USGA put the 14-club limit into effect in January 1938, with the R&A following 17 months later. (Sound familiar?) Prior to that, most touring pros were carrying at least 20 clubs. Harry Cooper had 26 in his bag when he won the 1926 Los Angeles Open. Lawson Little carried as many as 31 in the mid-1930s. The 14-club limit was imposed because golf's ruling bodies feared the game was becoming too easy.

As for preserving tradition, consider this: Harry Vardon carried six clubs through most of his career. Chick Evans used seven to win the U.S. Amateur and U.S. Open in 1916.

Greg Norman, Mark O'Meara, John Cook, Bernhard Langer, Butch Harmon and David Leadbetter were among several who dismissed my suggestion of an 11- or 12-club limit, saying it would make little difference in scoring.

"These players would adapt, they're so good," said Leadbetter. "They'd change lofts and sort out the arrangement."

Leadbetter reckoned the limit would have to be 10 clubs before scoring was affected, although he did concede that even a modest reduction "would make people hit some shots they wouldn't hit otherwise."

Tom Kite, Paul Azinger, Charles Howell III and Singh were among those who said reducing the club limit could have a significant effect on scoring, some figuring as much as a shot or two each round.

"Sure it would," said Kite. "It would make a big difference. The more limitations you put on players, the more you demand of them."

Traditionalists argue that setting different rules for tournament and recreational play would break the common thread that links golfers of every ability. The USGA and club manufacturers find themselves strange bedfellows on this point, because the latter hooks so much advertising on tour usage.

Let's get real. That common thread has been frayed for decades. Rarely does the average golfer play under the same conditions and with the same customized equipment as the pros. If a 10-club limit were implemented, and Joe Golfer still wanted to measure himself against the pros, what's to stop him from pulling four clubs out of the bag?

Those who care only how they stack up against Ralph, Roger and Ray on Saturday morning at My Home Country Club can stick with 14. Club manufacturers could still tout tour usage and still sell 14 clubs to 99.9 percent of the golf public. They might even benefit from a new niche market for 'tweener irons and other multipurpose sticks.

By now you're probably thinking, "What next, Dave? Bring back the stymie?"

Laugh if you like, but be advised that others who wield more influence than yours truly are thinking outside the box, too.

I ran the 11- or 12-club limit past Peter Dawson, secretary of the R&A.

"It might bring some shotmaking back," Dawson said, "but it still wouldn't affect distance off the tee. I like my idea better."

Which is?

"Ban the tee peg," he said. "Just drop the ball on the tee box and hit it from there."

Now that would be interesting.

**Architects:** John Brademus, 1935 • Perry Maxwell, 1940    **Superintendent:** Jeff Elliott, CGCS

# Colonial Country Club

## Fort Worth, Texas

A few minutes south of downtown Fort Worth, Texas, lies the Colonial Country Club, a perennial favorite venue on the PGA Tour. This long, demanding par-70 course was built in the midst of the Depression by an eccentric named John Brademus (1884-1946) and quickly became one of the South's most highly regarded facilities. In preparation for the 1941 U.S. Open, the club brought in Perry Maxwell, the genius of prairie golf design (Southern Hills and Prairie Dunes). In adding three holes, Maxwell refined Colonial's design balance so that no two holes run in the same direction and there is a good mix of those that bend left and right.

Most of the 5,500 square-foot bentgrass greens are open in the front and are designed to accommodate golf in a region where the winds can be severe. There are two heart-stopping exceptions where water is placed flush to the front of the green: the 402-yard ninth hole, and the 178-yard 13th. The fairways average about 32 yards wide, with the effective playing area pinched even more by mature pecan trees that come into play in the landing and approach zones.

The course is built on flat land, with no more than a 10-foot elevation change throughout the layout. Driving is especially taxing, what with dozens of fairway bunkers on the inside of doglegs. Further complicating the demands upon accuracy off the tee are the firm, fast fairways. At the 470-yard, par-4 fifth hole, for instance, it's not uncommon to see a ball land in the fairway and bounce so far to the right that it trickles into the Trinity River. That's one of many good reasons why 30 years ago this hole was selected by Dan Jenkins as one of "The Best 18 Golf Holes in America."

—*Bradley S. Klein*

| Par | 70 |
|---|---|
| Yards | 7,080 |
| Slope | 133 |
| Rating | 74.7 |

**Golfweek Rating**

**7.27**

# Newport Country Club

## Newport, Rhode Island

| Par | 70 |
| --- | --- |
| Yards | 6,735 |
| Slope | 129 |
| Rating | 72.7 |

*Golfweek* **Rating**

**7.26**

Few clubs have been more central to the history of American golf than Newport Country Club. One look at its ornate, Beaux Arts clubhouse tells you the world to which it belongs. The club was established in the late 19th century as a refuge for elite families summering on nearby Bellevue Avenue in Newport.

The club was a founding member of the U.S. Golf Association in 1894, and the next year hosted the first U.S. Open and the first U.S. Amateur. A century later, Newport was the scene of Tiger Woods' second Amateur title. In 2006, Newport is slated to host its first U.S. Women's Open.

The setting is incomparable—a wide-open, sandy site overlooking Rhode Island Sound. Today's incarnation of the course dates to a total makeover by Donald J. Ross, subsequently revised and partially rerouted by A. W. Tillinghast. Together, they created pure links golf holes that accommodate howling winds. The bone-dry fairways are ideal for low-slung approaches. Wayward golf balls or shots coming up short find deep bunkers, many of them pulled back slightly. That leaves awkward recovery shots over intervening mounds.

—*Bradley S. Klein*

**Architects:** Harry S. Colt & Charles A. Alison, 1929    **Superintendent:** Pat Sisk, CGCS

# Milwaukee Country Club

## Milwaukee, Wisconsin

Among the designers from the old world who shaped the golf landscapes of the new world were Englishmen Harry S. Colt (1869-1951) and Charles H. Alison (1882-1952). Chief among their skills was working with parkland sites, where heavier clay soils made for less than ideal golf conditions. The solution was to utilize existing surface contours for drainage while making sure those slopes also worked well for golf.

That's exactly what makes Milwaukee Country Club one of their more notable achievements. With returning nines that start and end at a central outlook point for the clubhouse, the course manages to make 90 feet of elevation change work without overwhelming the golfer. The ninth hole, a diagonal par-4 of only 332 yards, relies upon the native upslope to present golfers with alternative landing zones.

The back nine brush up alongside the Milwaukee River, gently incorporating it into play on five holes. The 375-yard, par-4 11th hole turns sharply left around a scattershot bunker complex; those who bail out or blow the drive through the fairway on the right face the prospect of trickling into the river.

Milwaukee Country Club hosted the 1969 Walker Cup (U.S. defeated GB&I) and the 1988 USGA Senior Amateur (won by Clarence Moore). For more than a half-century, the club's pro shop has been home to Manuel de la Torre, one of the game's legendary instructors. De la Torre began his run as head professional at MCC in March 1951. He was the first professional selected as the PGA National Teacher of the Year in 1986. You'll find him on "his tee" six days per week, sunup to sundown, May through October.

*—Bradley S. Klein*

| | |
|---|---|
| **Par** | 72 |
| **Yards** | 6,928 |
| **Slope** | 135 |
| **Rating** | 73.8 |

*Golfweek* **Rating**
7.25

# Valley Club
# of Montecito

## Santa Barbara, California

| Par | 72 |
|-----|------|
| Yards | 6,595 |
| Slope | 133 |
| Rating | 72.2 |

*Golfweek* **Rating**

7.24

The famed golf architect, Dr. Alister MacKenzie (1870-1934), was best known as a master of deception who relied on nature's beauty to hide the man-made elements in his golf holes.

With the Valley Club of Montecito, MacKenzie and his design partner Robert Hunter were given a site that evoked visions of old Spanish California. The site was framed with oaks, eucalyptus and sycamore trees and featured two small hills, 50 feet of elevation change in all. A series of creeks created natural-looking diagonal strategic options. MacKenzie also drew upon skills as former military camouflage pioneer to build bunkers that sometimes made the near look far and

other times induced a false comfort. These hazards rely on a charm that can best be described as hypnotic. Your attention is drawn to them, while your ideal shot should be played away. This unnerving form of deception isn't seen in most modern designs, where targets are readily defined.

A trip to the Valley Club is usually best saved for in the late afternoon and into the early evening hours, when glorious golf days are blessed with the sun setting on the Pacific Ocean, just one half-mile west of the back nine.

—*Bradley S. Klein*

**Architect:** A. W. Tillinghast, 1922    **Superintendent:** Robert U. Alonzi, CGCS

# Fenway Golf Club

## Scarsdale, New York

### Fenway Shares Spotlight with Tillinghast Elite

*By Bradley S. Klein*

For years, when golf conversation in New York's Westchester County turned to the works of A. W. Tillinghast, the names Winged Foot and Quaker Ridge rightly came up, but there the talk abruptly ended. Today, there's a third sibling in the mix—Fenway. Having three top 50 designs by the same classical architect within five miles of each other is an impressive achievement. That Fenway is part of the conversation today is attributable not only to its inherent design but also to a long-term restoration plan that has revived the layout's strengths after they lay obscured for decades.

Fenway emerged from a Broadway theater elite that in the 1920s would not settle for second best. They had a Devereux Emmet-designed course on hand, called Fenimore Golf Club, but only two years after it opened, the membership turned to Tillinghast for a complete redesign, and today's routing of Fenway arose in its place. The 140-acre parcel was relatively treeless in 1924, the only major routing constraint being a nine-hole short course, subsequently plowed under and now the site of parking, tennis courts and the practice field.

For decades, Fenway kept a low profile while its neighbors hosted major tournaments. But subtle changes also took hold, particularly years of tree planting and growth, as well as bunker deterioration or removal. Particularly significant was the loss of outlying putting surfaces through circular mowing practices and the encroachment of greenside rough. In this manner, some of the most interesting hole placements get lost. Such compromises of architectural integrity are imperceptible year

| | |
|---|---|
| **Par** | 70 |
| **Yards** | 6,722 |
| **Slope** | 130 |
| **Rating** | 73.0 |

**Golfweek Rating**

7.22

to year. But over time, they add up and take their toll—a commonplace occurrence at many older golf courses.

Things started to change in 1996, when a coterie of members decided to improve their golf course, not by modernizing but by restoring it. They brought in architect Gil Hanse, who drafted a long-term planning document that guided all subsequent work. Hanse based his interpretation on extensive historical data, including original engineering plans that bore Tillinghast's signature, dated January 25, 1924. Key leadership throughout the process has come from longtime green chairman Steve Frankel, who guided, cajoled and promoted the effort like a masterful politician getting a bill through Congress.

The master plan effort was enhanced halfway through when Fenway brought on board veteran superintendent Robert U. Alonzi, CGCS. His pedigree includes a legendary family affiliation in the greenkeeping business and extensive experience at other fine area clubs. Now, after years of watching other area clubs enjoy the limelight, Fenway is back at center stage.

## America's Best: Rater's Notebook

### 1. Ease and intimacy of routing: 7
Readily walkable thanks to efficient use of land. Site is tight, leading to many parallel holes, mostly on back nine and separated by tree lines.

### 2. Integrity of original design: 9
Routing is identical, as are green sites. Only concession to modern play is that in rebuilding older, flat-bottom bunkers with sodded, partly revetted walls, Hanse moved bunkers marginally to accommodate more modern play while preserving the classical cross-bunkering motif.

### 3. Natural setting and overall land plan: 6
Essentially a leafy residential community surrounds the property with the perimeter framed by mature trees. Views and sensibility of the grounds are thus oriented to the interior of the site.

### 4. Interest of greens and surrounding contours: 10
Fascinating set of diversely contoured greens, average size of 5,000 square feet. On many holes, Tillinghast created deception when the green is viewed from main approach area; he tucked a section of the putting surface off to one side and divided it visually from main body of green with a slightly raised mound or bunker face. The smaller section of green draws one's eye and tempts the golfer to go for it.

### 5. Variety and memorability of par 3s: 5
Quite the mix—the short, drop-shot fourth is followed by the full-bore sixth where the approach has to draw in over a perfectly placed carry bunker 30 yards short of the green. Both par 3s on the back nine are a bit miscast here. The 11th plays two clubs longer than the yardage owing to a 45-foot uphill climb to a landing area you can't see; by contrast, everything is visible on the 17th, though the pond fronting the green looks more like Florida than Westchester.

### 6. Variety and memorability of par 4s: 7
The greens and approaches differentiate these holes more than the tee shots. Great illusion on the parallel eighth and 12th, where a massive bunker fronts and divides two putting surfaces that appear to be unified. Miniscule putting surface on the 301-yard 15th is shaped like a charcoal briquette and is equally hard to hold.

### 7. Variety and memorability of par 5s: 7
Among the major restorations at Fenway was putting back the sprawling Sahara bunkers in the second-shot landing area of the third hole. The long 18th calls for a second shot through a tree-lined chute.

### 8. Basic quality of conditioning: 8
An ideal Northeastern presentation of turfgrasses, with a slightly old-fashioned rough that includes ryegrass, bluegrass and diverse fescues.

| Hole | 1 | 2 | 3 | 4 | 5 | 6 | 7 | 8 | 9 | Out | |
|------|-----|-----|-----|-----|-----|-----|-----|-----|-----|-------|---|
| Yardage | 290 | 455 | 523 | 148 | 475 | 245 | 390 | 353 | 400 | 3,279 | Card of the Course |
| Par | 4 | 4 | 5 | 3 | 4 | 3 | 4 | 4 | 4 | 35 | |
| Hole | 10 | 11 | 12 | 13 | 14 | 15 | 16 | 17 | 18 | In | Total |
| Yardage | 451 | 200 | 454 | 411 | 435 | 301 | 431 | 190 | 570 | 3,443 | 6,722 |
| Par | 4 | 3 | 4 | 4 | 4 | 4 | 4 | 3 | 5 | 35 | 70 |

**9. Landscape and tree management: 4**

They're making progress, but there still is a way to go in decluttering the grounds.

**10. "Walk in the park" test: 9**

Neat old club, with a charming first tee where everyone stops to watch you hit. From there until the 18th green, you feel like this is what a private club should be like today.

**Overall average of *Golfweek* raters: 7.22**

# Modern Courses

Shadow Creek Golf Club
*North Las Vegas, Nevada*

*Modern*
course profile

# Sand Hills Golf Club

## Mullen, Nebraska

| | |
|---|---|
| **Par** | 71 |
| **Yards** | 7,089 |
| **Slope** | N/A |
| **Rating** | N/A |

*Golfweek* **Rating**

**9.42**

Sand Hills Golf Club gained immediate attention throughout the golf world when it opened in 1995 for the simplicity—or "minimalism"—of its design. The only difference from pure linksland is that there's no ocean to be found. Nor, for that matter, is there a single lake or tree on the golf course, nor a flowerbed, hanging tee sign, arrows pointing the way around, dress code or cellular phone. What gives the course its power and character are the three central elements of links golf: sand, howling winds and firm turf.

Sand Hills sits near the town of Mullen (pop. 554) on the easternmost edge of the Mountain Time Zone. The 1,000 acres composing the golf course, clubhouse-lodge and overnight cabins on the banks of the Dismal River were part of an old ranch and still look that way. The private club derives its name from the surrounding terrain, 18,000 square miles of grass-covered dunes occupying the central quarter of Nebraska.

No written description of this stunning par-71, 7,089-yard golf course can do justice to its beauty or genius. The holes are framed by terrifying yet lovely golden grasses, and the greens are boldly contoured, with ample ground for run-up shots and multiple options for chipping. Best of all are the views, which on some holes extend to the horizon of the prairies. Massive natural "blowouts" of sand have been ingeniously incorporated as sand hazards. The effect is overwhelming.

*—Bradley S. Klein*

**Architect:** Tom Doak, 2001    **Superintendent:** Kenneth Nice

# Pacific Dunes

## Bandon, Oregon

Pacific Dunes, like its sister course Bandon Dunes, debuted near the top of *Golfweek*'s America's Best Modern list when it became eligible in 2002. Pacific Dunes is the exquisite handiwork of Tom Doak, described as "golf design's new minimalist Michelangelo" in a *Golfweek* profile of the Bandon experience.

Carts are not allowed at Pacific Dunes. Who wouldn't want to walk this ground? It overlooks Oregon's rugged coast and challenges the golfer with some of the most thoughtful contemporary architecture in the game.

Little earth was moved in the construction of Pacific Dunes. Six "natural bunkers" guided Doak's routing that zigzags amid the dunes and pine scrub immediately north of the Bandon Dunes course. The result was unconventional. There are seven par 4s on the first nine and only two on the back. The homeward nine has three par 5s and opens with two of its four par 3s. The slingshot-shaped ninth hole has two greens, an upper and lower. (A sign on the tee tells you which one is in play that day.)

Pacific Dunes features three par 4s under 350 yards. But don't be deceived by its relative shortness, at least by today's standards. The layout may be only 6,557 yards from the tips—and 6,174 from the tees most visitors should use—but every inch is a test. The greens are small, some with severe undulations, and judgment of the wind can make or break a round. Masters of the bump-and-run have a distinct advantage at Pacific Dunes.

This is a course for thinkers and shotmakers, not sluggers. If you aren't a purist before you arrive, you're likely to be one by the time you leave.

*—Dave Seanor*

| | |
|---|---|
| **Par** | 71 |
| **Yards** | 6,557 |
| **Slope** | 133 |
| **Rating** | 72.3 |

**Golfweek Rating**

**9.21**

**Architect:** David McLay Kidd, 1998    **Superintendent:** Troy Russell

# Bandon Dunes

## Bandon, Oregon

| | |
|---|---|
| **Par** | 72 |
| **Yards** | 7,212 |
| **Slope** | 150 |
| **Rating** | 76.8 |

**Golfweek Rating**

**8.53**

Bandon Dunes' destiny as one of America's very best was apparent in August 1998, when seven *Golfweek* writers were treated to a sneak preview of this stunning layout designed by a then-obscure Scottish architect named David McLay Kidd. At dinner during our second night in the rustic fishing village of Bandon, and after 36 holes of jab-filled match play, the group conducted a secret ballot of favorite holes and best holes on the new course. Seven different holes were selected as favorites; five different holes received votes as best.

Such is the overall strength of Bandon Dunes. And perhaps more significant, the group agreed that no hole could be rated as even marginally bad.

The slogan at Bandon Dunes is "Golf as it was meant to be played." This is a walking-only course, with a cadre of knowledgeable caddies on hand. There are no home sites on the course, and owner Mike Keiser vows there never will be. Stand just off the fourth green, on the edge of the 100-foot bluff overlooking the Pacific, and all you can see in either direction along the coastline is pristine dunes land, unspoiled beach and awe-inspiring rock formations.

Only a 100 years of history—and about 7,000 miles—separate Bandon Dunes from the legendary links courses of Scotland and Ireland. This is Oregon, so prepare for rain. Wind off the ocean might call for a driver to reach a 170-yard par 3. Greens are tucked into the nooks and crannies amid untouched sand dunes. Stacked sod bunkers dictate the angle of attack. Opportunities for the bump-and-run and knockdown 6-irons are there for the taking.

Kidd said his goal was not only to bring a true links experience to America, but also to provide "both a sense of adventure and an exploration of this great landscape." He succeeded on all counts.

**—Dave Seanor**

# Whistling Straits (Straits)

## Sheboygan, Wisconsin

The Straits course shows just how special something can be if you combine Herb Kohler's resources and vision with Pete Dye's artistry. The result is a masterpiece along two miles of Lake Michigan shoreline that will challenge the world's best players in the 2004 PGA Championship.

The walking-only, links-style course resembles something out of Ireland. Its rugged, windswept terrain, juxtaposed to adjacent flat farmland, is not an easy walk. Nor are its holes an easy play.

Dye started with a 560-acre parcel of flat land previously used as an army base, including runways for aircraft. Seemingly half the sand in Saudi Arabia was trucked in for dunes effect. The before-and-after pictures are more stunning than those from Hair Club For Men. "A once in a lifetime thing," Dye called the experience.

Because of wind that usually roars in off the lake, the Straits' fairways are 40 to 50 yards wide. Among the most interesting creations is the trouble to the left of the 389-yard, par-4 10th that resembles lunar landscape; there, a tee shot to a perched fairway with bunkers in the middle must be spot on.

Perhaps most memorable are the four par 3s. All sit along the coastline and are probably the course's most scenic holes. The last of these, the 223-yard 17th (called "Pinched Nerve"), has Lake Michigan sheer on the left and massive dunes short and right. That and the treacherous 18th will have a major say in who wins the 2004 PGA.

The course features fescue fairways, massive sand dune bunkers and views of Lake Michigan from all 18 holes. Its playing surface varies in elevation, from near lake level to panoramic bluffs 50 feet high. For the 2004 PGA, Whistling Straits should look a lot on TV like it does in person—overwhelming.

*—Jeff Rude*

| | |
|---|---|
| **Par** | 72 |
| **Yards** | 7,362 |
| **Slope** | 151 |
| **Rating** | 76.7 |

**Golfweek Rating**

**8.45**

*Modern course profile*

**Architect:** Pete Dye, 1994    **Superintendent:** Gary J. Grandstaff

# Pete Dye Golf Course

## Bridgeport, West Virginia

Designers don't put their own name on a golf course lightly, which is why Pete Dye took pains to get this one right. Design and construction took 15 years, more than 150 site visits, and more earth moving than he or anyone in the coal-mining country of north central West Virginia could ever account for. That's what it took to convert 235 acres of abandoned mining fields into some of golf's most visually overwhelming—and strategically sound—holes.

There are forced carries over rocky streams, paths that wind across antiquated wooden bridges, a walkway that carries golfers through a cold, dank mine shaft, a par 5 that lines up with 1,200-foot-high smokestacks in the distance, a sluice that tumbles out of the side of a green, and a putting surface located under an exposed 65-foot wall comprising the coal-laden Pittsburgh Seam.

Dye plays with your eye and with your mind. On many holes, you're tempted to go for distant landing areas that are diagonally arrayed across fearsome hazards; yet if you turn away and play a different angle the path becomes open and accessible. The greatest tease comes on the short, par-4 17th, where Dye provides a half-acre putting surface that's impossible to miss and impossible to putt. Take a closer look here and you'll spot a 4,000 square-foot "green within a green" that's the real target.

—*Bradley S. Klein*

| | |
|---|---|
| **Par** | 72 |
| **Yards** | 7,166 |
| **Slope** | 141 |
| **Rating** | 75.4 |

**Golfweek Rating**

**8.23**

**Architects:** Tom Fazio & Steve Wynn, 1990  **Superintendent:** David Diver

# Shadow Creek Golf Club

## North Las Vegas, Nevada

Here's a formula for a can't-miss golf course. Take a dead-flat site of 220 arid, unfertile acres. Create 100 feet of elevation change by deploying an army of bulldozers. Plant 21,000 trees at $1,000 apiece (landscaping item=$21 million). Add water and seed, and wait. Presto! A world-class golf course.

That's exactly what casino impresario Steve Wynn did in the late 1980s, in conjunction with Tom Fazio. They were intent on proving that the land doesn't matter if you have enough technology, imagination and money. In the process, they totally transformed expectations about what golf course architecture could do.

What a perfect theatrical drama they created against the natural backdrop of Sunrise Mountain and the Sheep Range. All this in a desert oasis of a city that has a Brooklyn Bridge, an Eiffel Tower and 2,000 Elvis impersonators. Why shouldn't a golf course be a stage production, too?

Best of all, it's open to the public, provided you stay at one of the MGM Mirage Corp.'s six hotels in town. And there's the little matter of a green fee—$500—but it includes the limo ride from the hotel and cart fees. Sorry, caddie gratuities are extra. But who goes to Vegas to scrimp on dreams?

**—Bradley S. Klein**

| | |
|---|---|
| **Par** | 72 |
| **Yards** | 7,239 |
| **Slope** | 138 |
| **Rating** | 73.0 |

***Golfweek* Rating**

**8.15**

*Modern course profile*

**Architect:** Pete Dye, 1967    **Superintendent:** Keith Kresina

# The Golf Club

## New Albany, Ohio

The Golf Club, in a northeast suburb of Columbus, Ohio, is among Pete Dye's most enduring works and certainly the one that brought national attention to him among serious students of architecture.

The course derives its character from a simple principle—in order to gain a sense of elevation, cut down to reveal features naturally, rather than build them artificially. That's precisely how Dye managed to create such a sense of drama and visual intensity on what is a rather low-profile expanse of farmland.

At the 369-yard, par-4 13th, Dye relied upon cut-down railroad ties to create distinct plateaus. At the 618-yard, par-5 14th, he uses a diagonal bunker on one side of the fairway and a marshy pond on the other by the second shot landing area to create great diversity of playing angles on what amounts to a straight hole.

—*Bradley S. Klein*

| | |
|---|---|
| **Par** | 72 |
| **Yards** | 7,266 |
| **Slope** | 140 |
| **Rating** | 75.3 |

*Golfweek* **Rating**
8.15

# Muirfield Village Golf Club

## Dublin, Ohio

| | |
|---|---|
| **Par** | 72 |
| **Yards** | 7,224 |
| **Slope** | 147 |
| **Rating** | 76.1 |

**Golfweek Rating**

**8.13**

The "House that Jack Built" in his hometown to play host to the PGA Tour's Memorial Tournament is a spectacularly successful product of a most unlikely collaboration. The design partnership between "the Bear and the Beard," Nicklaus and Desmond Muirhead, was short-lived, but in at least this case, amazingly fruitful.

Muirhead, who died in 2002, was an artist, land sculptor and airy visionary who primarily did Muirfield Village's routing. The returning nine sit side by side, each forming a counterclockwise loop that brings creeks and cross slopes gently into play. Many of the tee shots are ever so slightly uphill and leave downhill shots for approaches. Nicklaus, the meticulous, demanding, focused champion golfer, was responsible for strategy and feature work. Three decades later, he's still tinkering away, making sure this perfectly conditioned layout stays fresh and challenging to a new generation of golfers.

One of Muirfield Village's design innovations comes at the par-4 14th, a 368-yard stretch of broken dreams that single-handedly revived architectural interest in the value of the short two-shotter. Golfers here face a delicate approach into a narrow green, with bunkers on the left and a steep bank down to water on the right. For all of Muirfield Village's demands on power and aerial control, this deft little hole speaks volumes about Nicklaus's understanding of sound strategy.

—*Bradley S. Klein*

**Architect:** Lester George, 1999     **Superintendent:** Peter Wendt

# Kinloch Golf Club

## Manakin-Sabot, Virginia

### Kinloch a Welcome Throwback

*By Bradley S. Klein*

The golf world in staid Old Dominion has a newcomer on its hands that's already being talked about—rightly, in this reviewer's judgment—as the state's best course. Kinloch Golf Club, 12 miles west of downtown Richmond, is something of a throwback in an area of horse country that's fast becoming the frontier of residential development.

Luckily for golfers able to afford its pricey membership, Kinloch is an ideal refuge. This is a pure golf club. No swimming pool. No tennis courts. Kinloch is a walkable layout with well-trained caddies and, best of all, a stunning layout in pristine shape that provides plenty of optional routes of play.

Inspiration—and sweat equity—for the project came from amateur golf champion Marvin "Vinny" Giles. His résumé includes British Amateur and U.S. Amateur titles, participation on four Walker Cup teams and a Walker Cup captaincy. Now he has collaborated with course architect Lester George on a golf facility that takes the game to heart.

Kinloch, par 72, plays from 5,360 yards up to 7,168 (75 rating/138 slope). Befitting its simplicity, the names of the holes are one word and in each case suggestive of its design or location (Redan, Glade).

The setting is a rolling, 270-acre wooded site with 70 feet of natural elevation change. A massive lake bisects the property. The only limitation is a tight property line alongside the lake that forces a very long separation between nines. Carts are provided to bridge the gap, but after the 18th hole, golfers have the option of playing a par 3 across water to a green sitting right in front of the clubhouse.

| | |
|---|---|
| **Par** | 72 |
| **Yards** | 7,168 |
| **Slope** | 138 |
| **Rating** | 75.0 |

**Golfweek Rating**

**8.00**

# America's Best: Rater's Notebook

## 1. Ease and intimacy of routing: 6

Holes flow well, with short hikes from tee to green on each nine. First hole is awkwardly isolated alongside the range, and there are very long rides from ninth and 18th greens because of the 270-acre site being pinched at midpoint between a lake and the property line. But overall, it's comfortably snuggled in.

## 2. Quality of feature shaping: 9

Lovely tie-in of features, with no abrupt transitional areas. All ground rolls tied in to native grades.

## 3. Natural setting and overall land plan: 7

Expansive setting, a comfortable teaching center by the practice tee, and a clubhouse offers a view of a 70-acre lake. Each hole sits in its own corridor, but the tree clearing allows subtle looks below and through the canopies to give broader context of the course.

## 4. Interest of greens and surrounding contours: 8

Greens vary in shape, size and contouring, and Lester George is not afraid to let putting surfaces run out to the rear—but with enough up front to run the ball into them.

## 5. Variety and memorability of par 3s: 9

Clubs hit from middle tees: 6-iron, 7-wood, 9-iron and 3-wood. No forced carries across water, each green differently configured.

## 6. Variety and memorability of par 4s: 7

Dramatic, sometimes intimidating, with optional paths and two that offer split-fairway alternative routes (though both of these are early in the round and play left to right). Six of the par 4s play right to left, and two others (first and 12th) demand an approach shot shaped opposite to the drive. Very dramatic Cape hole at No. 16.

## 7. Variety and memorability of par 5s: 6

Interesting variety of options, especially at the 521-yard 11th hole, with alternative fairway left of stream bisecting the hole. However, the 586-yard ninth hole, called Palisade, is over-designed in terms of different routes, with an attractive look that is a headache to figure out.

## 8. Basic quality of conditioning: 9

Unbelievable for a new course. Flawless L-93 bentgrass greens; the same turfgrass, cut higher, offers an amazingly tight fairway surface that's ideal in the fall but requires lots of tender loving care and hand watering to keep healthy and firm in this hot summer climate. Bonus points for lining up the mowing stripes on the tees with the mowing stripes on the fairways.

## 9. Landscape and tree management: 6

Excellent clearing job and opening of understory, but a few too many trees near tee shots, and that "featured" hardwood on the 15th is excessive.

## 10. "Walk in the park" test: 8

A good caddie program, cart paths that are never in view (much less in play) and the occasional ability to spy on neighboring holes during a round all make for a welcome experience. Too bad about the cross-country hikes between nines.

**Overall average of *Golfweek* raters: 8.00**

| Hole | 1 | 2 | 3 | 4 | 5 | 6 | 7 | 8 | 9 | Out | |
|------|---|---|---|---|---|---|---|---|---|-----|--|
| Yardage | 442 | 400 | 540 | 334 | 194 | 407 | 237 | 437 | 586 | 3,577 | Card of the Course |
| Par | 4 | 4 | 5 | 4 | 3 | 4 | 3 | 4 | 5 | 36 | |
| Hole | 10 | 11 | 12 | 13 | 14 | 15 | 16 | 17 | 18 | In | Total |
| Yardage | 450 | 521 | 455 | 579 | 152 | 328 | 471 | 213 | 422 | 3,591 | 7,168 |
| Par | 4 | 5 | 4 | 5 | 3 | 4 | 4 | 3 | 4 | 36 | 72 |

# "This is a pure golf club."

**Architect:** Pete Dye 1983    **Superintendent:** David Stone

# The Honors Course

## Ooltewah, Tennessee

The Honors Course was envisioned by founder Jack Lupton as a place of refuge and as a tribute to amateur golf.

Designer Pete Dye psychologically whipsaws the player with holes that induce visions of double digits while other holes raise hopes of redemption.

The 17th hole, a 494-yard par 5, ascends to a steeply pitched pulpit green fronted left by a 12-foot deep bunker that would do C. B. Macdonald proud. Here, Dye employs his full arsenal of misdirection. Attempts to reach the green in two call for a high second shot faded from a hook stance. If you can play that shot, you can play golf.

Dye, ever mindful of how real golfers play, produced a course that is not anxiety-provoking when played from the middle tees. It was highly regarded by all contestants in the 1994 Curtis Cup, for example, when women amateur teams from the United States and Great Britain and Ireland played to a draw.

And yet it can be brutal. During the 1996 NCAA Championships here, Tiger Woods shot a final-round 80 and still won by three strokes. By the time the 2004 Southern Amateur and the 2005 U.S. Mid-Amateur set up shop, the course will be even tougher, thanks to new back tees adding 160 yards to the existing scorecard.

Still, there is much solace to be found at the Honors Course. Credit for the sanctuary-like atmosphere goes (in part) to David Stone, the only superintendent the Honors Course has ever had. In naturalizing the out-of-play areas, he relied upon a planting scheme he derived from studying abandoned farms in the area to see what grew as nature reclaimed them. He found that indigenous vegetation, such as blackberry and goldenrod weed, attracted varied wildlife, including bluebirds, wild turkey, piliated woodpeckers, fox and bobcat. No wonder taming the Honors Course has proven so difficult.

—*Bradley S. Klein*

| Par | 72 |
| Yards | 7,064 |
| Slope | 151 |
| Rating | 75.4 |

*Golfweek* Rating
7.93

# Making a Muni

## Building This Home Course Is a Personal Journey

### By Bradley S. Klein

If we knew more than eight years ago what we'd be in for, I doubt anyone in my town would have undertaken the project. And yet we managed to complete our Pete Dye/Tim Liddy-designed municipal golf course. Opening day was September 27, 2003. I was amazed that we were actually going to play the course. So was the whole town of Bloomfield, population 19,000, in north central Connecticut.

The focus of our collective ambitions has been Wintonbury Hills Golf Course. (Wintonbury was the town's name more than a century ago.) For years, the people behind the effort to build the course were subject to questions and doubts. Now, all who tour the site agree it's a stunning architectural achievement. The trouble we've gone through appears to be paying off. Not that we'd never do it again; thankfully, we won't have to.

Journalistic integrity requires that I confess my ongoing role in the project from the beginning. It started in October 1995 and picked up steam once construction finally got under way in March 2002. Officially, I'm co-chair of the municipal building committee and share duties with veteran golfer and fellow town resident Duane Haley. We all volunteered our time—a lot of it, as it turns out, what with meetings, site visits and hundreds of phone calls.

With the first tee only 3.2 miles from my front door, it was very tempting to take my dog, Divot, out there for a morning walk (armed, of course, with a pooper scoop). Lunchtime found me hanging out at the construction trailer or hiking out to look at ongoing work. By late afternoon I'd be tempted to take a quick look at the day's progress.

### Background

The golf course will come in at $11.5 million for everything, including land acquisition, engineering and design, construction, maintenance building, clubhouse and parking lots. That's a little more than the initial deal we struck with Dye, when he agreed to design the course for $1 (one of a handful of such "pro bono" projects he was undertaking in those days). Golf course construction was reasonable by industry standards and came in exactly at the budget we set—$5.05 million. The rest of the money went for land purchase, wetlands and soil studies, legal fees, engineering, maintenance equipment and the buildings.

Luckily, the town was able to raise money for the project through a general obligation bond at an interest rate of less than five percent. In an era when citizens regularly vote down swimming pools, new police stations and high schools, we were able to garner overwhelming public support on three different referendum votes over a five-year period.

The real trick always has been to keep the green fee affordable—$35 to $50 for town residents, including optional cart, with nonresidents paying about $15 to $20 more. We always planned some sort of discount for seniors and juniors, and we were determined to make the course walkable as well.

Town manager Louie Chapman Jr., who has shepherded the project along from the beginning, was adamant about the commitment to quality: bentgrass greens and fairways, a first-rate design with unimpeded long views, and a true public-access facility. The long-term goal was to draw visitors to Bloomfield while making the residents proud. If we can enhance the town's tax base by making Bloomfield a little more appealing, great. We also think we can make the golf course work as a business enterprise on its own.

## Site and Design

Armchair architects might think the design process is an intellectual affair, as if they could simply work on an uncluttered canvas and impose their art without constraint. In fact, most of what passes for golf course architecture today is problem solving of a highly technical sort. The real art lies in getting a site to work and keeping it playable, interesting and maintainable—all while tiptoeing through a stunning maze of obstacles involving budgets and government regulations.

Two years into the initial design process, the Connecticut Department of Environmental Protection ruled our first choice of a site as unacceptable. It was back to the drawing board—and to town maps in search of buildable land. That's no easy feat in a municipality that's 30 percent wetlands and where much of the remaining undeveloped land is in various land trusts or park systems.

We finally landed on the only acceptable tract in town—a 291-acre parcel, with 89 acres of wetlands scattered across it and a power line down the middle. Dye and Liddy went through a dozen different routing iterations and four years of meetings with engineers, wetlands experts and authorities from the town, state and the U.S. Army Corps of Engineers before final approvals came.

The result was a par-70 course, 6,620 yards from the back tees, returning nines, with the outgoing side looped in a tight clockwise and the incoming nine hooking around it on the outside. Everyone knew the highlight of the course would be the 455-yard 14th hole, a par 4 alongside a massive reservoir pond. The key was to make the other holes equally interesting without making golfers feel cramped by the various site constraints.

## Construction and Grow-in

The dust started flying in early 2002, when tree clearing and bulk earth work (230,000 cubic yards total) began. The identity and feel of a golf course don't emerge, however, until the fine features are inscribed in the ground in the form of bunkers, putting surfaces and surrounds. We were lucky to have on board a skilled feature shaper in Phil Coles. He can work a bulldozer like a surgeon with a scalpel. Liddy spent many hours during his nearly two dozen site visits getting Coles to abandon the soft, mounded look he was used to building and create Dye's trademark stark, lunar look.

Some designers are really salesmen. Others just want to create good golf holes. Liddy explained it best during a midsummer trek on the site.

"I hate putting on a suit and tie and going to meetings," he said. "I love wearing work boots and jeans and being out here on the ground."

During one marathon two-day visit in July 2002, Dye and Liddy dazzled the construction crew with a seminar in the fine art of detail work. They wanted fairway bunkers oriented toward the front of greens and greenside bunkers aligned with the back of greens. They made tiny adjustments in putting surfaces so that surface water rolled off one way while the ball's momentum might carry it in another. And they surprised others, as well as me, by insisting that all target areas—including putting surfaces—be visible from the approach zones.

Project manager Sean Noonan spent more than two years housed in a ramshackle construction trailer making sure the plans were properly followed. Grow-in was handled by superintendent Greg DuBois. He was formerly an assistant at Winged Foot Golf Club in Mamaroneck, N.Y. before leaving to oversee three complete grow-ins previous to Wintonbury Hills. We were lucky to land him and luckier to keep him on after opening.

Many years of planning. Frantic months of construction. Endless hours of preparation for the opening date. All of us involved in Wintonbury Hills know that the work and pride we put into the project have enabled us to build something special. All it takes is a walk down one of our fairways and a look around to the lake or to the distant hills to feel that it's all been worthwhile.

Before and after photos show how much work was needed to create playable holes at Wintonbury Hills Golf Course in Bloomfield, Ct. *Above*, the par-4 15th hole, 427 yards. *Below*, the par-4, 455-yard 14th hole, alongside a lake that had algae during construction. *Center*, the superintendent is usually the unsung hero. Here is Wintonbury greenkeeper Greg DuBois, left, with famed turf consultant Dick Bator.

**Architects:** Bill Coore & Ben Crenshaw, 2003     **Superintendent:** William E. Jones

# Friar's Head

## Baiting Hollow, New York

Modern *course profile*

Even in an area like Long Island that's so rich in classical course architecture, there is no comparable site to the 350 acres that Friar's Head occupies on Suffolk County's North Shore. The course looks out upon Long Island Sound and presents a powerful juxtaposition of wooded dunes and open farmland—no easy synthesis to weave together into a single, coherent golf experience.

Coore and Crenshaw took great pains to preserve the natural features of the site while massaging just enough roll and drainage into the lower-lying farmland areas. The result was a stunning debut in 2003 that earned Friar's Head *Golfweek*'s first annual award for best new course.

Some holes are built entirely in the wooded dunes; others sit on open farmland or transition between the two landscapes. The bunkers look like natural blowouts created by decades of erosion. The putting surfaces, built the old-fashioned

way as push-up greens from native mix, sit easily on the ground and take on the character of their native terrain. Wide fairways, such as at the 322-yard, par-4 5th hole, leave plenty of room for strategy. Here and throughout the course, divergent lines of play are accentuated by the brisk winds that are typical for the area.

There's also no shortage of visual deception in the placement of hazards and playing features. At the 207-yard, par-3 10th hole, Coore and Crenshaw had the temerity to place nearly a half-acre putting surface behind a native dune that obscures much of the green from view.

This is a course that respects the game's traditions and along the way evokes the genius of a Ballybunion or Cypress Point. Teeing grounds are uncluttered, with no hole signs or ball washers. If you need to find a yardage from the fairway, the only available help is not from a marked sprinkler head but in the form of a knowledgeable caddie.

—*Bradley S. Klein*

| Par | 71 |
| --- | --- |
| Yards | 6,965 |
| Slope | 144 |
| Rating | 74.1 |

**Golfweek Rating**

**7.92**

**Architect:** Pete Dye, 1981    **Superintendent:** Fred W. Klauk Jr.

# TPC at Sawgrass (Stadium)

## Ponte Vedra Beach, Florida

Think about it: By definition, can there possibly be such a thing as a terrifying golf shot from 132 yards? Most would say no—unless, that is, they have the occasion to walk onto the 17th tee of the Stadium Course at the Tournament Players Club at Sawgrass.

The equation is simple enough: Hit a good shot, likely with an 8- or 9-iron, and putt for birdie; miss the green, listen for a splash, and start figuring real quick how many golf balls you have left in the bag. Here's one guarantee: every ensuing swing gets a little bit tougher.

Bottom line: You may be there awhile.

Sure, the TPC at Sawgrass is famous for its oft-photographed, smallish but devilish 17th hole and all the pain it brings even the best players of the world once a year at the PGA Tour's venerable Players Championship. But there is much more to the golf course, a masterpiece that creator Pete Dye terms "a place that just has a feel about it."

The 455-yard 14th is a pretty straight line from tee to green, but the contours of the fairway make for a double dogleg of sorts, bending right and back to the left. It calls for a long fade off the tee with the driver to a two-tiered fairway. Miss the green with an approach, and bunkers and grass bunkers tucked amid mounds make for a tricky up-and-down proposition.

The closing hole, the 440-yard 18th, is hardly a breather for those surviving the treacherous little approach at 17. The 18th calls for a long, gentle draw off the tee and likely a mid-iron to an undulating putting surface. Water guards the left side of the hole—the entire quarter-mile.

The TPC at Sawgrass generally is regarded as the best of the PGA Tour's TPC family of courses. It only seems to get better with age. Its champions include everyone from Jack Nicklaus to Greg Norman to Tiger Woods, the latter having won both a U.S. Amateur (1994) and a Players Championship (2001) on the property.

*—Jeff Babineau*

| Par | 72 |
|---|---|
| Yards | 6,954 |
| Slope | 138 |
| Rating | 73.3 |

*Golfweek* **Rating**

7.83

Modern
course profile

# Cuscowilla
# on Lake Oconee

## Eatonton, Georgia

At Cuscowilla, course designers Bill Coore and Ben Crenshaw have crafted an exquisitely understated residential development. The holes are routed effortlessly over undisturbed land, and the distance from green to tee is never more than a few steps.

At 6,847 yards, the par-70 Cuscowilla layout is not long by modern standards. Four native farm ponds come into play, and two holes sit along Lake Oconee. In line with traditional golf values, the landing areas are generously wide and there's never a forced carry approach. As Crenshaw noted at an opening day fete, "You can't beat golfers over the head with problems they can't solve."

Nowhere are options better presented than at Cuscowilla's fifth hole, a slightly uphill, 305-yard par 4 with a double fairway that wraps around a gaping 70-yard crevice of sand that ends short of a hump-backed green. The hole brings to mind Alister MacKenzie's scruffy-edged handiwork, yet takes his famed No. 12 hole at Royal Melbourne's Championship Course in Australia a step further by introducing an optional landing area to the left.

Bunkers don't do all of the work of strategic definition here. In clearing and shaping Cuscowilla—the site used to be an experimental nursery; all the specimens are tall, sturdy and upright—Coore and Crenshaw allowed a number of pines to come into play, though in every case there's an optional route. The high leaf canopies of these conifers leave plenty of space underneath for imaginative recovery shots.

—*Bradley S. Klein*

| | |
|---|---|
| **Par** | 70 |
| **Yards** | 6,847 |
| **Slope** | 132 |
| **Rating** | 72.2 |

*Golfweek* Rating

7.81

**Architect:** Robert Trent Jones Sr., 1966  **Superintendent:** Chris Dalhamer

# Spyglass Hill Golf Course

## Monterey, California

Spyglass Hill Golf Course, finished in 1966, remains a Robert Trent Jones Sr. masterpiece, at least in part because of a striking contrast to its acclaimed neighbor, Pebble Beach Golf Links. Whereas Pebble Beach runs along the coastline and through adjacent open areas with sparse trees, Spyglass Hill offers a tantalizing taste of the coast and then meanders through meadows and the dense Del Monte Forest. The diversity of Spyglass Hill is stunning.

The course starts on a dramatic note—a 595-yard par 5 that literally tumbles down toward the beach. The next few holes bring the coastline into view, if not into play. The aesthetic culmination of the round comes early, at the fourth hole, a sweeping dogleg-left par 4 of 370 yards, which hangs on the edge of a coastal marine platform that's strewn with sand and ice plants. At the sixth tee, a par 4, the course heads into the forest, never to return to sea.

Spyglass, like Pebble, is open to the public. Its back-tee yardage, 6,862, can be very misleading. Owing to damp conditions, the course generally plays extremely long. Statistics from the AT&T Pebble Beach Pro-Am show that, for PGA Tour players, Spyglass Hill has been more difficult than Pebble Beach in the last several decades. Playing Spyglass Hill is a test not to be taken lightly.

Because the Monterey Peninsula is one of the premier golf destinations in the world, Spyglass Hill is assured of retaining high visibility. Side by side, Spyglass Hill and Pebble Beach are one of most intriguing one-two combos in golf.

—*James Achenbach*

| | |
|---|---|
| **Par** | 72 |
| **Yards** | 6,862 |
| **Slope** | 148 |
| **Rating** | 75.3 |

**Golfweek** Rating
7.79

**Modern** course profile

**Architect:** Tom Fazio, 1988    **Superintendent:** Tom Bailey

# Wade Hampton Club

## Cashiers, North Carolina

| Par | 72 |
|---|---|
| Yards | 7,154 |
| Slope | 136 |
| Rating | 74.4 |

**Golfweek Rating**

**7.79**

The key to a successful golf community lies in the land plan. At Wade Hampton, 3,500 feet above sea level in the Blue Ridge Mountains of western North Carolina, the golf holes are routed on softer terrain while the houses are scattered around the perimeter and look down upon the course. The 300 home sites on the 700-acre property all adhere to a restriction that guided development: "Whatever is necessary for playing golf."

The land was the former summer haunt of a legendary Confederate general (later South Carolina governor, then senator) by the name of Wade Hampton III. Dense woods, rocky outcroppings and a lovely stream give character to the land. So does the towering presence to the immediate east of 4,700-foot tall Chimney Top Mountain.

The true genius of modern architecture is fitting playable holes upon rugged land. Here, Tom Fazio managed to create holes that complement the character of the site and yet appear softer than the surrounds. The course varies in elevation by 110 feet. Most of the holes play downhill, with the climbs reserved for the walks from green to tee.

The holes sit well here and highlight the native terrain. Fazio saved the most dramatic vista for the penultimate hole. The 196-yard, par-3 17th sits in a little valley, with two fir trees providing goal posts for the tee shot. At first glance, you find the target inviting, but then as your eyes scan behind the green and work their way upward, you suddenly feel overwhelmed by the exposed granite face of Chimney Top looking down upon you.

*—Bradley S. Klein*

# Ocean Course at Kiawah Island

## Kaiwah Island, South Carolina

Two things spring to mind when Pete Dye's Ocean Course at Kiawah Island comes up in conversation: Its proximity to the Atlantic and its degree of difficulty. Ten holes are laid out along the ocean, and the sea is in view from all 18. Its beauty, however, can't mask its uncongeniality toward visitors who arrive without their "A" games.

The Ocean Course, venue for the 1991 "War by the Shore" Ryder Cup Matches, ranks among the toughest courses in the United States. The slope and rating listed are from the tournament tees, and the corresponding numbers are 73.4/139 from the 6,552-yard championship tees and 71.1/133 from the 6,031-yard guest tees.

The Ocean Course owes its difficulty to the way Dye pocked the property with bunkers and snaked the layout among dunes and marshes. Water frequently comes into play. Recovery from its many shaved greenside runoff areas requires the deftest of short games.

In 2001, Dye returned and oversaw revisions that made hazards more visible on the second and fourth holes. He also added drama to the 18th by moving the green to the right and closer to the ocean.

Unchanged is the notorious 17th, the 210-yard par 3 over water where Mark Calcavecchia hit arguably the worst pressure shot in golf history. Leading his Ryder Cup singles match 4 up with four holes to play against Colin Montgomerie, Calcavecchia lost the last four, a meltdown lowlighted by his cold top off the tee at the 17th, a shot that barely made it halfway into the pond. The United States ultimately regained the Cup by a score of 14 1/2 to 13 1/2 when Bernhard Langer, playing Hale Irwin in the final singles, missed a six-foot par putt at the 18th that would have beaten Irwin and won the Matches for Europe. Calcavecchia didn't see the gripping finish. Convinced he had blown it for his teammates, he was alone on the beach, sobbing.

—*Dave Seanor*

| | |
|---|---|
| **Par** | 72 |
| **Yards** | 7,296 |
| **Slope** | 144 |
| **Rating** | 77.2 |

*Golfweek* **Rating**
7.73

**Architect:** Tom Fazio, 2002    **Superintendent:** David C. Denley

# Dallas National Golf Club

## Dallas, Texas

Architect Tom Fazio is legendary for working design wonders with nondescript sites. Usually he does it by building everything from scratch. Halfway into the front nine at Dallas National, however, you realize that not even Fazio could have created the whole site himself. Instead, he got his hands on an astonishingly good piece of land and managed to make it even better.

It took course founders/developers John MacDonald and Mike Letchinger of Potomac Golf Properties years of study and regulatory wrangling to convert this geologically quirky 388-acre site into a mature parkland layout. Although owned by a mining company, it had never been quarried. Real estate development was a no-no thanks to city zoning ordinances governing subsurface escarpment areas.

So the land lay unused for years until MacDonald and his partners cultivated their vision of a private club devoted single-mindedly to golf. Now the site looks more like Northern New England or Napa-Sonoma wine country than hardscrabble central Texas. And yet here you are, only six and a half miles southwest of downtown Dallas, on rolling uplands with vast stands of mature hardwoods, stream beds, dramatic ravines, and 160 feet of elevation change on a wondrously playable site.

Exposed limestone walls come into play on two long holes, the 475-yard par-4 8th hole and the 245-yard, par-3 17th. Golfers are also treated to a handful of challenging carries across a deep ravine that winds through the grounds. There is wide berth given to lines of play and great diversity of playing angles and teeing grounds.

Dallas has always been a great sports town, but it has not measured up to other major American cities when it comes to quality golf course design. Perhaps that's why it hasn't hosted a professional major since 1963. Dallas National now gives this city what it had lacked—a muscular, high-quality golf course capable of hosting a U.S. Open.

—*Bradley S. Klein*

| | |
|---|---|
| Par | 72 |
| Yards | 7,326 |
| Slope | 155 |
| Rating | 76.1 |

**Golfweek Rating**

7.72

# Wolf Run Golf Club

## Zionsville, Indiana

Wolf Run is the legacy of the late Jack "Wolfman" Leer (1929-1995). A dentist by trade, he was an accomplished golfer of national amateur ranking, including an Indiana state amateur title on his resume. The man he relied upon to design the course, Steve Smyers, played on the legendary University of Florida golf team with Gary Koch, Andy Bean and Phil Hancock that won the 1973 NCAA championship. Design work has not stilled Smyers's competitive skill; he has gone on to make match play in several U.S. Amateurs, Mid-Amateurs and British Amateurs.

A look down the Wolf Run's first fairway conveys a clear sense of what this private club 16 miles north of Indianapolis is all about. Those who are into "do or die" heroics will need to play somewhere else. Here, the seductions are of a subtle nature. From the elevated tee of this 375-yard par 4, a set of diagonal bunkers on the left side is directly in play. There's plenty of room wide right for a safe opening drive, but that leaves a bad approach angle to a tightly bunkered green. Dare to play the bold line left, and the second shot in is much easier. Miss it a tad, and punitive fescue rough lies in wait, as well as gnarly, old-fashioned-looking sand.

The bentgrass putting surfaces, at an average size of 5,000 square feet, are not modest in their contours. They also vary dramatically according to the demands of the hole, with the short par-4 seventh green only 2,300 square feet and the long par-3 13th green more than five times that size.

No one would mistake Wolf Run for easy. The fairways are on the tight side, averaging 32 yards in width. This is not a course for every golfer. It's only for those who respect the game's traditions and who appreciate what refined shot-making entails.

*—Bradley S. Klein*

| Par | 71 |
|---|---|
| Yards | 6,926 |
| Slope | 143 |
| Rating | 74.2 |

*Golfweek* **Rating**
7.66

ModernCourseFeature

**Architects:** Dan Proctor & Dave Axland, 1999    **Superintendent:** Josh Mahar, CGCS

# Wild Horse Golf Club

## Gothenburg, Nebraska

### Wild Horse Offers Affordability, Quality

*By Bradley S. Klein*

Great public golf courses in the $30 range are all the rage, in no small part because of the success of the 2002 U.S. Open at Bethpage State Park's Black Course. If the U.S. Golf Association is serious about its commitment to affordable, high-quality golf, it should venture westward to the great American prairie and find a suitable championship for Wild Horse Golf Club in Gothenburg, Nebraska. The town used to be famous for its Pony Express station. Now it merits national attention for a course ranked No. 19 on *Golfweek*'s America's Best list of modern courses.

Credit goes to Dan Proctor and Dave Axland for this down-home, rugged heartland layout built on old grazing ground. The two soft-spoken, aw-shucks guys are proprietors of a modest little design-and-build outfit called Bunker Hill Golf Inc., based (sort of) in Paxton, Nebraska. They started as shapers for Ben Crenshaw and Bill Coore and were largely responsible for the work at Sand Hills Golf Club in nearby Mullen. They applied the same restraint and respect for existing natural contours at Wild Horse. "We didn't move hardly any dirt," said Proctor.

The 330-acre golf course development, complete with a modest 5,500 square-foot clubhouse and 52 housing lots, cost less than $3 million to build. How can you not love a place where the lots (each one about three-quarters of an acre) were priced from $8,000 to $14,000? Talk about a land rush.

The par-72 course stretches to 6,805 yards (73 rating/125 slope), though three more forward sets of markers (down to 4,688 yards, 67.7 rating/108 slope) assure playability for an unusually diverse group of regulars—everything from worldly jet-setters to novices in cutoffs, tank tops and sneakers.

| Par | 72 |
|-----|-----|
| Yards | 6,805 |
| Slope | 125 |
| Rating | 73.0 |

**Golfweek Rating**
**7.63**

Wild Horse sits 2,200 feet above sea level on the southern edge of the vast Sand Hills region. The arid climate is ideal for links-style golf, aided by winds that regularly howl 20-30 mph throughout the golf season, which runs March through November.

Green fees are $30 on weekdays and $35 on weekends (plus optional cart on a very walkable layout). That's expensive by local standards but cheap for those accustomed to rates at East or West Coast "country clubs for the day."

This one beats them all, with both fine golf and memorable atmosphere. Local membership might be the greatest deal in the history of golf: $450 annually, plus a $500 initiation fee payable over five years. For another $200 per year, members, their immediate families and their guests get all the cart use they can handle.

## America's Best: Rater's Notebook

### 1. Ease and intimacy of routing: 8

Returning nines, each contiguous and looped in a basic counterclockwise pattern. Front nine is basic; back nine is much stronger. Walking paths through native grassland make for an easy route to follow. Holes sit naturally on existing contours.

### 2. Quality of feature shaping: 6

What feature shaping? Proctor and Axland rototilled what was there, tossed some seed down and called it a golf course. Guess that means the Big Guy upstairs shaped it all—and very well, too, since the rolls and slopes steer the ball around better than any bulldozer-made features could have.

### 3. Natural setting and overall land plan: 6

Rolling grasslands, surprisingly bold slopes at times and a sense of remoteness just approaching the place via I-80. A frontier ambiance prevails in the clubhouse, where one big comfy vaulted room serves as pro shop, snack stop and bar. My only concern is what things will look like when those houses go up along the perimeter. At least they're not planned for inside the golf course.

### 4. Interest of greens and surrounding contours: 6

Bentgrass greens averaging 6,000 square feet get a little intense at times, as do large greenside rolls into bunkers or chipping areas.

### 5. Variety and memorability of par 3s: 5

Front nine par 3s are a letdown, but back nine pair varies admirably, with the 126-yard 11th hole playing uphill to a tight landing area and the 208-yard 13th offering lots of options off the tee.

### 6. Variety and memorability of par 4s: 6

Holes play shorter than their length because of altitude, firm fairways and wind. Landing areas are very wide, which allows for loads of cross-hazards that are in play and force golfers to play strategically.

### 7. Variety and memorability of par 5s: 8

Front nine par 5s rely largely on twisty native contours. Back nine par 5s are ingenious for their flexibility, thanks to loads of mid-fairway bunkers.

### 8. Basic quality of conditioning: 6

Fairways and tees are Kentucky bluegrass and perennial rye. Collars are fine fescue. Roughs are native prairie grasses. What a lovely alternative to the laser-edged, Botox green and white-flashed sand look of too many modern courses. Lean, mean, nasty and firm, plus the occasional spottiness as well—a welcome alternative thanks to restraint and sensibility by the staff.

### 9. Landscape and tree management: 9

Tree management is easy; there isn't one out here. Knee-high buffalo grass can get frustrating, but it looks great, especially when it waves in the wind.

### 10. "Walk in the park" test: 8

Real golf here: Folks carry their own bags or use pull carts, and families play golf together. The tee sheet is multicultural: a foursome of jeans-clad drinking buddies who whoop it up will be followed by well-coiffed, Gucci-toting men of leisure who just stepped off a Lear jet. The air is fresh and clear of allergens. The sky is big and blue. Why can't more course planners keep it this simple?

**Overall vote by Golfweek course raters: 7.63**

| Hole | 1 | 2 | 3 | 4 | 5 | 6 | 7 | 8 | 9 | Out | |
|---|---|---|---|---|---|---|---|---|---|---|---|
| Yardage | 328 | 431 | 537 | 171 | 367 | 548 | 364 | 451 | 155 | 3,387 | Card of the Course |
| Par | 4 | 4 | 5 | 3 | 4 | 5 | 4 | 4 | 3 | 36 | |
| Hole | 10 | 11 | 12 | 13 | 14 | 15 | 16 | 17 | 18 | In | Total |
| Yardage | 408 | 126 | 442 | 208 | 524 | 342 | 445 | 505 | 418 | 3,418 | 6,805 |
| Par | 4 | 3 | 4 | 3 | 5 | 4 | 4 | 5 | 4 | 36 | 72 |

*Modern course profile*

**Architects:** Tom Weiskopf & Jay Morrish, 1999    **Superintendent:** Bo Cichuniec

# The Rim

## Payson, Arizona

The Rim Golf Club is the answer to a trivia question: What was the last course designed by the dream team of Jay Morrish and Tom Weiskopf?

The course, opened in 1999, lies 75 miles northeast of Phoenix. Its setting is 5,000 feet above sea level in central Arizona's Mogollon Rim Country—one of the most spectacular spots in the arid Southwest.

Characterized by dramatic elevation changes among the largest stands of ponderosa pine in the United States, the Rim's routing plan is a spectacular combination of dense woods and scrubby manzanita brush in rocky, mountainous terrain.

Highlights include No. 8, a 225-yard par 3 that requires a forced carry over a mountain lake, and No. 13, a reachable par 5 that is one of the most memorable holes in the West. Beside the 13th green are awesome 80-foot-high boulders.

**—James Achenbach**

| Par | 71 |
| --- | --- |
| Yards | 7,193 |
| Slope | 139 |
| Rating | 73.4 |

**Golfweek Rating**
**7.59**

# Movers and Shapers
## Builders Instrumental in Giving Course Life

### By Scott Kauffman

Like a grown kid playing in the dirt, Dave Gandell maneuvers his John Deere bulldozer back and forth on a barren strip of land, shaping mounds of dirt as if he were building giant sand castles. Nearby, two chocolate Labradors are chasing each other and rolling around in the dirt.

For several months, this was the scene at the Brentwood First Tee facility. It's as if this once-neglected industrial area—a nine-hole golf course/practice range on the outskirts of downtown Jacksonville, Florida—had become a giant playground for Gandell and his dogs.

Welcome to Dave's World. Here, and at hundreds of other ongoing U.S. construction sites, the golf industry gets its start or rebirth.

"It sounds more glamorous . . . but I'm just a dirt hauler like the next guy," says Gandell, in reference to his position as a shaper with MacCurrach Golf Construction, one of the leading golf course builders in the country. "I love it. I love going out there and seeing a flat piece of land, taking a piece of dirt and helping interpret the architect's vision."

Job freedom is one of the bigger attractions. No bosses constantly looking over your shoulder. Just you, Gandell says, and the lay of the land.

"I come in in the morning, fire up my machine and just take off," says Gandell, one of two shapers on this MacCurrach Golf project.

Allan MacCurrach III, president of the company, remembers the rush of hopping on a bulldozer.

"When you put a 14-year-old on a bulldozer, it's a big world," says MacCurrach, now 40.

MacCurrach, whose father was one of the PGA Tour's first agronomists, got his start in the golf construction/maintenance business working for Pete Dye in high school in

1980. His first job was helping build TPC at Sawgrass in Ponte Vedra Beach, Florida, No. 12 among *Golfweek*'s America's Best modern courses.

"I picked up sticks in a five-gallon pickle bucket for $2.15 an hour," MacCurrach says. "Eventually, I graduated from picking up sticks to raking dirt. I raked the third green at the Stadium Course."

A year later, Dye offered MacCurrach a job to help build The Honors Course in Ooltewah, Tennessee, ranked No. 10 on the modern list. That was when MacCurrach learned to run a bulldozer and realized what he wanted to do in life: build golf courses.

After earning a two-year degree in turfgrass management from the University of Massachusetts in 1985, MacCurrach established his own golf construction company in 1987. Today, MacCurrach Golf is one of about 50 such companies in the country.

MacCurrach's firm is credited with building or renovating more than 100 courses, most of which are east of the Mississippi River. The company has built courses for some of the industry's biggest names, including Tom Fazio, Jack Nicklaus and Dye.

Two of MacCurrach's recent projects include the TPC at Virginia Beach and the Dye course at PGA Village in Port St. Lucie, Florida.

"So, in 20 years, I've gone from picking up sticks for the Tour to being the general contractor on a $6 million job," says MacCurrach, whose company has been ranked among the top construction companies—based on feedback from developers, architects and superintendents—each of the past 10 years by an industry publication.

According to MacCurrach, his company typically does eight to nine projects per year—five of which are usually new constructions—with a team of employees. MacCurrach's staff triples during summer months.

MacCurrach says the golf construction business is far from glamorous. And it can take its toll.

"You're on the road six to eight months [a year] . . . it's like a vagabond lifestyle," MacCurrach says. "It's just so taxing. A lot of these guys have made huge sacrifices. They're doing it for four or five years and all they can afford is a new truck.

"There's not many in the business that last four or five years. A lot are doing it for a short stint."

One common thread throughout the company, and the industry for that matter, is the understanding that course builders always will play a secondary role to the designer or architect. There are no MacCurrach "signature courses" being advertised.

"We're the unsung hero," says Chris Hill, one of MacCurrach's senior shapers at Brentwood.

Nonetheless, MacCurrach appears comfortable in his back-seat builder's role.

"As a contractor, one thing that really comes naturally is . . . you have to be truly willing and understand your part," MacCurrach says. "And be satisfied with the back seat. The architect's going to get it [publicity], and I have no problem with that.

"When I was working with Pete [Dye], I made a decision [that] to make a true impact, the construction business was where it was at. And I don't clean up too good. . . . So I'm better off playing this role."

What does the role entail? Typically, it means spending anywhere from 18 to 24 months on a new course construction site. On an extremely fast project with few problems, MacCurrach says he can have a new course ready for play in 11 to 12 months. That is taking into consideration seven to eight months for construction and four months of perfect grow-in conditions. But ideally, a builder prefers and needs an additional six to 12 months.

Usually, the first step in building a course is clearing the land. Then, the heavy earthwork, or the "cut and fill" process, begins. Next is two to three months of rough shaping, where dirt is moved based on the architect's plans.

Once the rough look of the course's tee boxes, fairways and greens are in place, the complex drainage and irrigation system is laid. Typically, this course lifeblood comprises 30 miles of pipes and valves.

Finally, the course undergoes a stage of finish shaping. Then it's time to plant grass.

The cost of a typical 18-hole course can vary based on many factors. For instance, different climates affect the length of the construction process, the grassing dates and the complexity of elements such as irrigation and drainage. Moreover, the physical characteristics of the site—such as topography, vegetation and soil conditions—also will affect costs. Lastly, government regulations, fees paid to designers, engineers and land planners, and the land's price can affect the bottom line.

Typically, however, when building an average 18-hole course, one can count on paying the following ranges, according to the Golf Course Builders Association of America: Designer or architectural fees might run as little as $150,000 or as much as $1.5 million for Nicklaus or Fazio "signature course" status. Course construction then can cost $4 million to $6 million.

The most important factor in building an affordable, accessible project, architect Michael Hurdzan says, is carefully choosing a site. The better the site, Hurdzan adds, the lower the construction and long-term maintenance costs.

Does MacCurrach have a preference for an architect or region of the country?

"If it's a sound site, a good owner and good architect…you put all those ingredients together, and I'm real happy," he says.

MacCurrach concedes that he likes building simpler courses.

"I don't like these humpty-dumpty courses," he says. "I don't like to build these courses where you need Dramamine to get through the first tee."

Whatever the case, MacCurrach has more than enough work. And there appears to be no end in sight to the construction boom.

According to the National Golf Foundation, more than 500 new courses opened in 1999, the first time course openings surpassed 500 in the industry's history (the number includes reconstructions), and then reached a 15-year peak in 2000.

But the economic downturn and the terrorist attacks of September 11, 2001, brought the boom to a halt. In 2002, approximately 248 courses opened, 38 percent below the 2000 mark and 13 percent fewer than 2001.

Bill Kubly, president of Landscapes Unlimited Inc., says he feels the industry has reached a plateau.

"I don't think there's going to be more work," says Kubly, whose Lincoln, Nebraska, company has built or renovated more than 200 courses in the last 10 years.

"We peaked at 500 a year," said Kubly. He foresees being at 200-250 annualy for the next few years.

Even so, that's approximately double the amount of new courses Kubly and his contemporaries were building in the 1970s, he says.

"At that time, I thought we'd be through in 10 years," Kubly says. "Thank goodness I was wrong."

Gandell is certainly grateful for it. Otherwise, he wouldn't have his day in the dirt.

## Cost to Build a Course

After site selection, here are typical capital budgets for two distinctly different levels of 18-hole championship courses with a driving range/ learning center. The 2003 estimates range from low end ($25-50) green fees to high end ($75 or more).

| PROJECT/ELEMENT | LOW END (130-150 acres) | HIGH END (200 acres) |
|---|---|---|
| Mobilization | $30,000 | $75,000 |
| Site clearing *(40-100 acres@$800-4,000/A)* | 32,000 | 400,000 |
| Selective thinning *(10-40 acres@$1,200-4,500/A)* | 12,000 | 180,000 |
| Grubbing and disposal | 5,000 | 10,000 |
| Major drainage | 75,000 | 500,000 |
| Minor drainage | 50,000 | 150,000 |
| Topsoil stripping | | |
| (a) 75,000 cubic yards | 100,000 | — |
| (b) 150,000 cubic yards | — | 200,000 |
| Earth moving *(including lake excavation)* | | |
| (a) 250,000 cubic yards | 375,000 | — |
| (b) 750,000 cubic yards | — | 1,500,000 |
| Topsoil replacement | | |
| (a) 75,000 cubic yards | 100,000 | — |
| (b) 150,000 cubic yards | — | 200,000 |
| Rock blasting *(if necessary)* | — | 150,000 |
| Greens construction *(100,000-140,000 square feet)* | | |
| (a) California spec | 240,000 | — |
| (b) USGA spec | — | 600,000 |
| Tee construction *(100,000-140,000 square feet)* | | |
| (a) topsoil spec | 30,000 | — |
| (b) amended soil spec | — | 140,000 |
| Driving range/learning center | | |
| (a) excavation/grading | 15,000 | 150,000 |
| (b) lights/structure | — | 240,000 |
| Irrigation system | | |
| (a) heads(400-1,000) | 400,000 | 1,000,000 |
| (b) pump station/pump house | 80,000 | 125,000 |
| Seedbed preparation(90-150 acres) | 95,000 | 150,000 |
| Seeding/sprigging(90-150 acres) | 90,000 | 150,000 |
| Sodding *(25,000/100,000 square yards)* | 50,000 | 200,000 |
| Straw mulch(90-150 acres) | 45,000 | 90,000 |
| Bunkers | | |
| (a) edging/contour | 20,000 | 40,000 |
| (b) sand purchase/placement | 50,000 | 120,000 |

| PROJECT/ELEMENT | LOW END (130-150 acres) | HIGH END (200 acres) |
|---|---|---|
| Bulkheading/Walls | 50,000 | 120,000 |
| Cart paths | | |
| (a) 12,500 linear feet tees/greens | 100,000 | — |
| (b) 30,000 linear feet wall-to-wall | — | 400,000 |
| Bridges *(as needed $100-300/lf)* | 30,000 | 100,000 |
| **CONSTRUCTION SUBTOTAL** | **2,074,000** | **6,990,000** |
| | | |
| **Parking(1.5 acres)** | **90,000** | **90,000** |
| Clubhouse *(high variable)* | | |
| (a) 4,000 square feet@$75 square foot | 300,000 | — |
| (b) 10,000 square feet@$200 square foot | — | 2,000,000 |
| Maintenance center *(5,000-8,000 square feet)* | 200,000 | 750,000 |
| Maintenance equipment | 350,000 | 1,000,000 |
| Landscaping | 10,000 | 250,000 |
| Establishment/maturation | 100,000 | 250,000 |
| Erosion control | — | 150,000 |
| Fees | | |
| (a) feasibility | — | 25,000 |
| (b) course architect | 250,000 | 1,250,000 |
| (c) project management | — | 210,000 |
| (d) civil engineering | 75,000 | 250,000 |
| (e) other*(see note 2)* | 80,000 | 1,000,000 |
| **OTHER SUBTOTAL** | **1,455,000** | **7,225,000** |
| | | |
| **TOTAL CAPITAL BUDGET** | **3,529,000** | **14,215,000** |

**Notes:**

**1.** Some golf course projects are being built for perhaps 30 percent less than the low estimate, if the site is near perfect. On the other hand, some "high roller" projects in the United States have exceeded the high estimate by 500 percent. The figures are only planning guidelines and should be adjusted for each particular site.

**2.** Some sites may require extensive and unique professional services, particularly when dealing in fragile environmental areas with complicated laws or regulations, or remedial engineering such as for earthquake or landslide protection.

**3.** The low-end course is based loosely on a course that might occupy 130-150 acres, would likely be less than 7,000 yards and would have a basic practice range, while the high-end course could be more than 7,000 yards and have a more elaborate practice facility.

**Source: Hurdzan/Fry Golf Course Design, Columbus, Ohio.**

*Architect:* Pete Dye, 1988 & 1990      *Superintendent:* Jeff Wilson

# BlackWolf Run (River)

## Kohler, Wisconsin

*Modern course profile*

At Blackwolf Run's River Course, Pete Dye worked with a rough piece of steeply elevated ground traversed by the Sheboygan River. With the river influencing play on 11 holes, it's good advice to play this from one of the three markers ahead of the back tees. Dye, more than any other architect, builds courses that crucify the golfer playing from the wrong starting point.

The opening holes are peppered with hummocks and exaggerated Scottish-style swales. Pot bunkers, wickedly contoured greens, and specimen trees on the insides of doglegs all conspire to make each hole memorable.

The ninth hole, a par 4 that stretches only 337 yards, is set on a broad plain alongside the river. A stand of 90-foot-high cottonwoods forces the golfer to carve a tee shot. The hole seems almost as wide as it is long.

Dye has held nothing back. The fairway at the 560-yard, par-5 16th hole unfolds like a battle plan. The putting surface, protected by an ancient linden tree, is perched so dangerously above the river 30 feet below that a golfer intently surveying a putt might well fall over the edge.

The 469-yard, par-4 final hole at the River Course turns elegantly left toward an enormous green. In late afternoon, the corrugated fairway creates a dramatic, shadowy effect. Gracing the scene from a rise well above the putting surface is a Canadian lodgepole pine clubhouse.

—*Bradley S. Klein*

| | |
|---|---|
| **Par** | 72 |
| **Yards** | 6,991 |
| **Slope** | 151 |
| **Rating** | 74.9 |

**Golfweek Rating**

7.52

# Kingsley Club

## Kingsley, Michigan

When Northern Michigan started its furious golf boom in the early 1990s, a handful of young, aspiring architects broke ranks with the heavily manufactured style then in vogue across the country.

Among those who sought inspiration from more traditional sources was Mike DeVries, formerly a maintenance crew member at nearby Crystal Downs, Alister MacKenzie's masterpiece. DeVries, a student of classical design, apprenticed with Tom Doak and Tom Fazio, then did some renovation work before getting the green light to implement his ideas on a blank slate. DeVries did not disappoint. Kingsley, a private club south of Traverse City, is retro all the way, with an opening tee shot brazenly evoking MacKenzie's "in your face" fairway bunkering at the 4th hole of Royal Melbourne's West Course.

From there to the 18th green, Devries supplies a roller-coaster ride of firm ground game features, wispy bunkers, and dramatic side slopes alongside multiple playing routes. The perimeter of the site is heavily wooded, but the playing character of the wide holes is all links thanks to bone-dry fescue fairways. Kingsley has far more slope and elevation change than any links course. Every shot here, whether a drive or putt, is moving along three dimensions.

The amazing thing is that DeVries moved only 30,000 cubic yards in the process—nothing compared to modern conventions, and yet the end product is a series of eye-popping, lacey bunkers that guard boldly sloped greens and approach areas.

The course has become a favorite of traditionalists and folks who appreciate the ground game. Two years running, Kingsley has hosted the national Hickory Open, for players using pre-1935 clubs.

—*Bradley S. Klein*

| Par | 71 |
|---|---|
| Yards | 6,723 |
| Slope | 132 |
| Rating | 73.1 |

*Golfweek* Rating

7.48

*Architect:* Tom Fazio, 1993    *Superintendent:* Mike Swinson, CGCS

# World Woods Golf Club *(Pine Barrens)*

## Brooksville, Florida

World Woods is an extraordinary public facility with two Tom Fazio-designed 18-hole courses, as well as a nine-hole short course, a three-hole practice layout and a 23-acre range.

The Pine Barrens course at World Woods opened in 1993 and quickly became a favorite among golfers who wish to push their games to the limit. The course also attracts many players who want to see if this layout really resembles famed Pine Valley Golf Club.

Whereas most Pine Valley wannabes have come up woefully short, Pine Barrens proves engaging and visually stimulating. "The closest thing to Pine Valley other than Pine Valley," said television analyst and former U.S. Amateur and British Amateur champion Steve Melnyk.

Fazio has designed a captivating mix of short and long par 4s at Pine Barrens. The first priority of every golfer there is to avoid the sandy waste areas that are present alongside every hole. The golfer who drives the ball accurately and intelligently will have a tremendous advantage here, especially if he chooses wisely and executes as planned.

The 494-yard, par-5 fourth and the 547-yard, par-5 14th offer generous bailout areas juxtaposed against tempting long targets for the bold player. Likewise, the 330-yard, par-4 15th, where those who choose not to try driving this downhill hole can lay up well short or play 30 degrees to the left of the tee. The choices are made all the more meaningful because the greens are large and well contoured, leaving much room for different angles of approach.

Visitors to this popular daily-fee facility also have the opportunity to play Pine Barrens' sister course, a faux Augusta National layout called Rolling Oaks. Together, they compose what is arguably the country's boldest experiment in architecture for a 36-hole public course.

*—James Achenbach*

| Par | 71 |
|---|---|
| Yards | 6,902 |
| Slope | 140 |
| Rating | 73.7 |

*Golfweek* **Rating**

7.47

# Pete Dye
## Genius, Not Always by Design

**By Bradley S. Klein**

Pete Dye stands at a podium in front of 1,000 people. It's mid-February 2003 in Atlanta. Most of those in attendance have been in town all week for the annual meeting of the Golf Course Superintendents Association of America. Now they are bedecked in suits and black tie for the gala dinner at which the greenkeepers present their highest honor, the Old Tom Morris Award.

Forty of Dye's (former) design associates and construction crew members have come in for the day. They had earlier feted him at a private reception. Now their mentor is about to step to the podium, having been introduced by Greg Norman, who flew in that afternoon for the celebration.

Dye, 76, doesn't look nervous. You'd never know that he's on the mend from colon cancer. He glances back at his wife of 53 years, Alice, then shuffles some odd papers on which he's jotted notes for his talk this night. In a few seconds, he's off on a stem-winder of a speech. It's part country sermon and partly a hilarious confessional of a failed greenkeeper. He holds nothing back, taking on the U.S. Golf Association, the folks who run The Masters, and spoiled golf pros who expect perfect lies every time. "You are the stewards of the game," he tells the superintendents. "You should run the game of golf."

### An Icon of Design

He's the architect who listens to no one, yet he has trained more disciples than anyone in the business. Dye infuriates clients, at the same time winning their lifelong friendship. He's the kindest man in the game when it comes to his time, yet no one revels more in making people suffer when they step onto his courses. People love him or hate him—usually both.

What's not to respect in a designer whose game is good enough to have qualified him for a U.S. Open? He knew Sam Snead, Donald Ross and Ben Hogan, and he played golf against Jack Nicklaus. He has nine layouts on the *Golfweek* America's Best list of top 50 modern courses, including four in the top 10. He has two sons, Perry and P.B., in the design business. And his wife, Alice, is a successful designer in her own right, as well as a Curtis Cup team member and two-time winner of the USGA Senior Women's Championship.

Not bad for a former insurance salesman.

Pete Dye, the game's Marquis de Sod, is the only course architect ever to outspend an unlimited budget. He's the man who won't—or can't—work from a topographic map and whose written plans come after the fact, to document what he did in the field.

"We had numerous extended conversations," said Dick Youngscap, who hired Dye in 1982 to build Firethorn Golf Club in Lincoln, Nebraska. "It was the only low-budget project he did in those days, and we both worked hard to make sure the course worked within those limits.

"He'd walk through these woods, and you couldn't see 15 feet around. But he kept seeing these golf holes. It's like he had the whole property map in his head. He knew exactly where all the boundaries were. And here it is 20 years later and we're on good terms. I even stay at his house when I'm visiting him at Casa de Campo in the Dominican Republic. So I guess all that fighting was worth it."

It has been said that Dye is more sculptor than architect, responding to his own creations—usually by changing them, often after they've been grassed. If he works instinctively, by feel, he also surpasses his colleagues in imagination and creativity. That's what has enabled him to fashion a pantheon of world-class courses, including Harbour Town Golf Links in Hilton Head Island, South Carolina (No. 24), the TPC at Sawgrass (Stadium Course) in Ponte Vedra Beach, Florida (No. 12), Pete Dye Golf Club in Bridgeport, West Virgina (No. 5), and Whistling Straits in Mosel, Wisconsin (No. 4), which will play host to the 2004 PGA Championship.

Dye's iconographic landscapes have imprinted themselves on the minds of modern golfers—many of whom lie awake at night replaying their tortured encounters with his railroad ties, island greens, boxcar bridges, 16-foot-deep greenside bunkers and 300-yard-long ponds. Nobody is better at tempting golfers to go for landing areas they have no business attempting. He doesn't build blind holes or features—he throws them in your face and dares you to play the short side of the hole, invariably the one flanking all of the danger. He usually also gives you lots of room to play safely, if you're smart enough to turn away and play there.

## An Early Path

It took a while for Dye to figure out his life calling. Born in 1925 in Urbana, Ohio, he picked up the game at age three. He had free run of nine-hole Urbana Country Club, a course his father, Paul Dye, built with some friends. Dye remembers working on the maintenance crew when he was seven years old. At first, he helped water the course, then mowed greens and fairways. By the time World War II arrived, Dye was recruited as the club's greenkeeper, a post he held while attending high school until 1944, when he signed up as an army paratrooper.

He was stationed at Fort Bragg in Fayetteville, N.C. When the commander asked if anyone could tend the base's course, Cpl. Dye stepped forward. Within two weeks, he and three officers were making regular afternoon trips 20 miles away to a resort named Pinehurst. There they played golf, much of it on Pinehurst No. 2, and had long talks with resident golf professional and course designer Donald Ross.

During his army days, Dye began drinking routinely. His father had been what Dye calls "a functional alcoholic." Gradually, Dye began to follow. The steady drinking continued for nearly 30 years.

"I was never to the point where I couldn't get out of bed and go to work, but that doesn't mean I wasn't an alcoholic," said Dye. His drinking continued until the early 1970s. He went to Alcoholics Anonymous, though the visit was to help an unnamed close acquaintance. Dye immediately realized that the symptoms described all pertained to himself.

"Walked out of there and never had a drink since," he said.

After World War II, Dye majored (briefly) in business at Rollins College in Winter Park, Fla. That's where he met Alice O'Neal, the lead golfer on the women's team. The two married in 1950, then both went to work as agents for Connecticut Mutual Life Insurance. She became the youngest member of the quarter-million-dollar round table. He was the youngest member of the million-dollar round table. His sales strategy was simple.

"I played golf all summer and never once mentioned a word about insurance," Dye said. "Then I'd put the clubs down on Labor Day and, over the next few weeks, call everyone I had played golf with. Sold like crazy."

He also played like crazy—with a flat swing and a draw that enabled the ball to run. He qualified for match play three times at the U.S. Amateur. In 1956, he played an exhibition match at Urbana CC against Sam Snead and a 16-year-old phenom from Columbus named Jack Nicklaus. Dye qualified for the 1957 U.S. Open at Inverness Club in Toledo, Ohio, where he shot 75-77 and missed the cut by two shots. The next year he won the Indiana Amateur, then went to the Trans-Mississippi Amateur at Prairie Dunes Country Club in Hutchinson, Kansas, where he played against Nicklaus.

"Lost 4 and 3, or something. If I'd beat him, it would've changed the whole history of golf," Dye said with a smile. "He would've gone home and I would've turned pro."

Instead, Dye turned architect. He long had dabbled in turfgrass and design, including some work at the Country Club of Indianapolis, where Dye was green chairman. During his tenure, the club lost 4,000 trees, many of them to Dutch elm disease. Dye planted new trees everywhere, something he regrets today. The club also was adjusting to its first fairway irrigation system and dealing with crabgrass that had infested its bluegrass fairways. Dye called upon experts at Purdue University in search of agronomic solutions. Among Dye's innovations was construction of a putting green that was the first in the country to meet what would soon become USGA specifications.

In 1959, Pete and Alice landed an unpaid design job, for the nine-hole El Dorado Golf Club in Indianapolis. They built the course themselves, grassing the greens with sod from their front lawn that they hauled in the trunk of their car. Their first paid assignment came the next year, an $8,000 fee for Heather Hills Golf Club in Indianapolis, with 18 holes squeezed onto 80 acres.

More jobs followed, enough to lead Pete away from insurance. (Alice had quit earlier in order to raise their two small boys.)

In 1963, he and Alice took a month-long tour of classical Scottish venues, a trip that changed their outlook entirely. At Prestwick, for instance, they discovered railroad ties shoring up the bunkers. Elsewhere, they found smallish greens, tiny pot bunkers, sprawling waste areas strewn with sand and a wide variation in playing conditions owing mainly to the wind. They also found greens with five to six feet of vertical slope. Dye says he measured everything, "so when people accused me of being crazy, I could tell them they did it that way in Scotland."

In 1964, he put together a syndicate of Indianapolis businessmen to create Crooked Stick Golf Club in Carmel, Indiana, a facility that went on to play host to the 1991 PGA Championship and the 1993 U.S. Women's Open.

Then came what remains his most sophisticated work, The Golf Club in New Albany, Indiana (No. 7). There he used gracefully shaped fairways and diagonally arrayed, low-slung bunkers to create multiple angles for shotmaking. The course, opened in 1967, continues to beguile golfers today as an example of using modest vertical contour to create powerful imagery and definition.

## An Era of Innovation

In planning Harbour Town in the late 1960s, Dye saw what Robert Trent Jones Sr. was doing a few miles away and simply did the opposite. Instead of huge, landing-strip tees, Dye built smaller teeing grounds. Rather than 9,000 square-foot, multilayered greens, Dye built them half that size and with virtually no contour. This on a site that offered exactly four feet of natural elevation. There are greens at Augusta National with more vertical relief. With masterful shaping and the use of railroad ties, sharp edging and ornamental flourishes of bahia and pampas grasses, he was able to create enduring holes that register themselves on the minds of golfers.

Whereas contemporaries such as Jones, George Cobb, Joe Finger, Dick Wilson, Joe Lee and George Fazio were emphasizing power, length and strength, Dye built a course entirely oriented around finesse. Harbour Town stood as a complete repudiation of that era's design style.

Many in the business probably wish that Dye had stuck with the subtlety of Harbour Town. Instead, he has tended to welcome the challenge of a succession of clients to build severe, totally artificial courses. "Of course they're unnatural," he says. "They have to be. If they were natural, you wouldn't be playing golf on them."

The best Pete Dye courses? Several candidates stand out. The Teeth of the Dog course at Casa de Campo in the Dominican Republic has features seemingly drawn with a surgeon's knife. No mechanical earth-moving equipment was employed. A throwback to the classical era, it was built entirely with hand labor.

## Enduring Landscapes

The innovative work continued with the PGA West Stadium Course in La Quinta, California, a layout that opened in 1986. Dye built a course in the middle of a barren, dead, flat desert spawning a real estate revolution. His Brickyard Crossing at Indianapolis Motor Speedway (1994) incorporates electric towers, railroad tracks, petroleum storage tanks, an on-site motel and the infield of the world's most famous racetrack. He started the Ocean Course at Kiawah Island, S.C., in 1989 on a hurricane-devastated beachfront under the considerable pressure of knowing it would debut two years later as host of the Ryder Cup.

With dozens of courses to his credit, Dye has been highly regarded enough by his peers that they elected him president of the American Society of Golf Course Architects—and then awarded him the Society's highest honor, the Donald Ross Award, at its 1995 meeting in Scotland. He also has something of a soft heart when it comes to taking on people interested in learning the trade. Among the designers who got their starts wrestling trees on Dye's construction crews are David Postlethwaite, Lee Schmidt, Bill Coore, Jason McCoy, Bobby Weed, Tom Doak, and of course, Dye's two sons, Perry and P.B.

Dye's designs turned the tables on power golf. His work reclaimed linksland traditions, resurrected the ground game, and adapted classical golf to the playing characteristics of modern balls and clubs. Along the way, he came to rely—perhaps too heavily—upon contrivance. But that may have been the only way to give undistinguished land some definition and character. His designs are extreme, but they are true to his vision.

In life and in art, the cutting edge—by its very nature—teeters on the brink. Living on the edge creates innovation, but it also takes a toll. The challenge of a creative soul is to know when to step back and keep one's art—and life—under control.

Pete Dye has done that, perhaps not always by design.

*Modern* course profile

**Architect:** Pete Dye, 1970    **Superintendent:** Gary T. Snyder

# Harbour Town Golf Links

## Hilton Head Island, South Carolina

There are green complexes at Augusta National with more elevation change than can be found on the entire site of Harbour Town Golf Links. When Pete Dye got to this low-lying site along Calibogue Sound in the late 1960s, he visited what Robert Trent Jones Sr. was building on Hilton Head Island and saw big tees, big fairways and big greens. Dye, ever the contrarian, did exactly the opposite at his course.

As a resort course, Harbour Town gets a lot of play, and as you start off you wonder why. It opens in a disarmingly simple way with greens so modest you wonder if you're playing the right course. Gradually, the pace quickens, and by the time you get to the 332-yard, par-4 ninth hole with its tightly bunkered, heart-shaped green, you realize you're in a special place.

The back nine accelerate the intensity, with the drama compounded by the overhanging canopies of live oak that drape the approach areas. The 373-yard par-4 13th is infamous for its railroad sleeper bunker fronting the tiny platform green. A pot bunker behind the green at the par-3 14th looks too small to take a swing in. The dogleg left par-5 15th demands Hoganesque shotmaking skills just to reach in three. And the play up the 18th hole, with the red and white lighthouse in the distant background, makes everyone feel like they've just come through a gauntlet.

—*Bradley S. Klein*

| | |
|---|---|
| **Par** | 71 |
| **Yards** | 6,973 |
| **Slope** | 146 |
| **Rating** | 75.2 |

**Golfweek Rating**

**7.46**

**Architects:** Rick Smith & Warren Henderson, 1999    **Superintendent:** Paul Emling

# Arcadia Bluffs

## Arcadia, Michigan

| Par | 72 |
|---|---|
| **Yards** | 7,404 |
| **Slope** | 143 |
| **Rating** | 75.1 |

**Golfweek Rating**
**7.41**

Few architects have the vision of Rick Smith, and he made the most of his imagination at Arcadia Bluffs. Created in the style of an Irish links course, Arcadia Bluffs occupies 245 windswept acres overlooking Lake Michigan. There is no housing on the property, but there are 50 sod-walled bunkers, expanses of native grasses and cavernous "natural bunkers" that blend seamlessly into the dunes land.

Arcadia Bluffs features 225 feet of elevation change from its highest point to the bluff, which itself is 180 feet above the beach. Smith's unusual routing features three par 5s and three par 3s on the outward nine. No. 9 is a stunning, 190-yard par 3 (240 yards from the tips), where the tee shot must carry a deep ravine and the green—guarded by front and side sod-walled bunkers—sits on the edge of the bluff.

There are plenty of opportunities for those who prefer the bump-and-run. True to its Irish motif, Arcadia Bluffs features a couple of blind shots, although the original quirky blind approach to the 18th was eliminated before the 2003 season by reducing the height of the mound that's 50 yards short of the green on the right side.

With views of Lake Michigan from nearly every hole, Arcadia Bluffs may well be the most distinctive links experience this side of Ballybunion.

—*Dave Seanor*

*Modern course profile*

**Architect:** Jack Nicklaus, 1981    **Superintendent:** Marshall Fearing

# Castle Pines Golf Club

## Castle Rock, Colorado

| Par | 72 |
|---|---|
| Yards | 7,594 |
| Slope | 155 |
| Rating | 77.4 |

**Golfweek Rating**

7.34

Television cameras give golf fans throughout the nation a chance to view Castle Pines Golf Club each year when it hosts The International. And even though the visuals are stunning, television just can't do justice to this course situated in the Rocky Mountain foothills.

Castle Pines perennially is listed as either the No. 1 or No. 2 course in Colorado (sharing the spotlight with Cherry Hills Country Club, which has hosted three U.S. Opens and two PGA Championships). And it is recognized as one of the most well-maintained venues on the PGA Tour.

The 10th hole draws the most attention, both for its beauty and its degree of difficulty. The hole originally was designed by Jack Nicklaus as a par 5, but Castle Pines founder/president Jack Vickers convinced Nicklaus to make it a stern, 485-yard par 4. Nicklaus agreed, making No. 10 a par 4 and switching No. 17 to a 492-yard par 5. The elevated tee shot at No. 10 is struck toward Castle Rock and the second shot sails toward Pikes Peak.

Other highlights at Castle Pines, which is situated at 6,400 feet in elevation with Ponderosa pine-lined fairways: No. 1, a 644-yard, dogleg left with a 180-foot elevation drop from tee to green; No. 9, a 458-yard par 4 that features waterfalls and ponds along the right side; and No. 12, a 422-yarder that requires a drive through a chute of trees and a green protected by a colorful bed of flowers.

—*Jeff Barr*

# Paa-Ko Ridge Golf Club

## Sandia Park, New Mexico

Please excuse the regulars at New Mexico's young word-of-mouth phenomenon, Paa-Ko Ridge Golf Club. They try not to gloat, but it's difficult when you're paying a mere $39 for a weekday walking green fee ($18 for carts) at the country's 23rd finest modern course, while dozens of bagtag-famous landmarks beneath Paa-Ko Ridge easily cost three times as much.

They perhaps could be more humble if these lands of the ancient Anasazi, located 20 miles east of Albuquerque in the Sandia Mountains, did not enjoy crisp, 80-mile views of five unspoiled mountain ranges or were blighted by fairway McMansions. Maybe the Paa-Ko regulars would hush up if they had to endure crowded five-hour rounds and greenside suburbia. But deep within the pinon and juniper canyons of Paa-Ko there are moments of such profound solitude that the only

sounds a golfer may hear will be the high desert wind and one's own beating heart.

At Paa-Ko, a Tiwa Indian word for "root of the cottonwood," two golf calendar par 3s drop more than 100 feet. Altogether here, a dozen tee-box vistas make you fumble for your camera.

What makes architect Ken Dye's work so superior to many other mountain courses is that each hole presents a carefully crafted challenge—a three-tiered, 100-yard-deep green here, a yawning arroyo there, and more perfectly placed pines, rock outcroppings and fairway bunkers than you'll see in a year. Bring your brain, and don't be intimidated. Dye doesn't try to punish 98 percent of the golf world just so you'll remember his name (first and last, that is). Solid golf is rewarded here from any of five tees.

—*Bradley S. Klein*

| | |
|---|---|
| **Par** | 72 |
| **Yards** | 7,562 |
| **Slope** | 138 |
| **Rating** | 75.2 |

***Golfweek* Rating**

7.32

**Architects:** Tom Weiskopf & Jay Morrish, 1991   **Superintendent:** Todd Voss

# Double Eagle Golf Club

## Galena, Ohio

John McConnell believes in doing things right. The founder of Worthington Industries (and the owner of the Columbus Blue Jackets NHL franchise) wanted a golf club, not a country club for his native Columbus, Ohio, area. No tee times. Something that would complement the region's great courses but that would look very different. There was one other thing he told co-designers Weiskopf and Morrish. "I'd like you to build me the Spectacles bunkers," McConnell instructed.

The 340-acre site he located 15 miles north of town had so much character that the builders, Wadsworth Construction, only had to move 300,000 cubic yards of dirt. Half of the holes on the heavily wooded front side utilized a 30-foot deep ravine.

The par-71 layout offers tremendous flexibility. Multiple options abound—none more compellingly than at the 355-yard 17th, where a massive fairway is split by sand and trees and the putting surface is the largest on the course. Imaginative shaping of Double Eagle's 82 bunkers recalls the design flair of Stanley Thompson. The greens, averaging 8,400 square feet, are not steeply decked and offer subtle contour.

The Spectacles work well, too, as fore bunkers that define the line to the ninth green. The result is a course that stands on equal footing with other Columbus-area greats including The Golf Club, Muirfield Village and Scioto.

—*Bradley S. Klein*

| | |
|---|---|
| **Par** | 71 |
| **Yards** | 7,100 |
| **Slope** | 138 |
| **Rating** | 74.3 |

**Golfweek Rating**

**7.31**

# Going Out on a Limb About Trees

## By Bradley S. Klein

Any time an eager host tells me how great the trees on his course are, I know I'm in for a nightmare. Invariably, I find holes that are stuffed and claustrophobic. Ironically, I often find trees that are much in need of care. That's because most so-called tree huggers have no idea what they're talking about. For the health and safety of the course, such neophytes should be kept as far away as possible from the grounds.

To start with, there is a proper place for trees on golf courses. Trees are fine on the perimeter of the property to screen out ambient noise and unsightly structures. They are ideal when allowed to flourish in dense clusters that can attract diverse wildlife. And trees are acceptable on the golf grounds when out of the way, such as behind a tee or alongside areas of play—but only when they are on the north or west side of areas that need to be maintained as turfgrass. And also only when they are the right kinds of trees.

People forget that trees need to complement and support the dominant function of the site, which is to enable golf to take place. As long as trees assume this secondary identity, they deserve tender, loving care. But when they become the dominant element in the land plan and more important than agronomy and golf course strategy, it's time to rev up the old McCullough chain saw and go to work on serious decluttering.

The problem lies in a fundamental conflict between trees and turfgrass. Both plant systems are competing for water, air, sunlight and nutrients. One of them is going to win. Usually it's the tree. When it does, turfgrass quality suffers and the grounds start going bare. Or the turf is starved, becomes susceptible to disease and needs to be treated chemically.

Trees on the east or south side of turfed areas are especially problematic, as they prevent precious morning sun from getting through. Without proper warming up and drying out, turf suffers. When shade covers greens, fairways or tees for large parts of the day, the plant leaf doesn't properly dry and photosynthesis is impeded. That's when conditioning declines.

Classical course designers never made trees central playing elements of a golf hole. Alister MacKenzie, Donald Ross and A. W. Tillinghast were influenced enough by links golf to know that ground game elements should prevail. They provided generous clearing plans on wooded sites. If trees have come to be major factors on their courses, it's because of years of overgrowth and generations of aggressive tree-planting programs.

"Don't touch those trees," says the member who joined in 1975. "They've always been there." Well, they might have been there for three decades, but photographic evidence from an earlier era usually will show a site that was windswept and virtually treeless. Or at least it will show holes of far greater width and lateral playing character.

After the first generation of members died off, family members and friends got the idea of honoring their dear departed with memorial plantings. It's bad enough to have a plaque affixed to them (making it tough to remove the tree). Far worse are those memorial trees with bricks or stone markers in the ground that the poor superintendent has to maintain.

American elms were an ideal golf course tree. They had high canopies under which light and air could pass. They were deep rooters that didn't impede cart and mower traffic. And they could be played around or under by golfers needing to escape from the rough. When Dutch elm disease wiped out these hardwoods in the 1950s and '60s, clubs started planting replacement trees like crazy. All too often the successors they chose were cheap species (white pines, swamp maples, pear trees, willow trees) that were ill-suited for the soil type or climate, were surface rooters rather than deep rooters, exuded bark and other debris, and were a constant maintenance and playability nightmare.

Trees have a funny habit of growing. That means they need to be monitored, trimmed and culled. Proper tree management is a costly undertaking. Trees constantly need to be evaluated for a number of things, including health, effect on agronomy, safety (especially weak limbs or leaning trees), aesthetic impact and consequences for course strategy.

A course that has fairways lined with trees has no strategic variety. It's also a course that unduly favors the long-hitting low-handicapper and unfairly punishes mid- to high-handicappers. Scratch golfers can hit the ball high, enabling them to get over trees. They also tend to benefit from the soft, wet fairways common on tree-lined courses. High-handicappers are doubly hampered by tree-lined fairways.

Peeling back trees has an amazing effect. Course conditioning invariably improves as the turf dries out, is healthier and produces deeper roots. Playability also is enhanced as golfers are provided with more lateral options. For low-handicappers, the course gets a little harder because the added ground roll takes their ball onto peripheral areas. Higher-handicappers benefit from more distance through ground roll, as well as more shot-making options for recovery.

Aesthetically, golfers also become more aware of their surrounds. Long views are opened up, creating new perspectives and a better sense of visual contrast. All of which makes for a more enjoyable round.

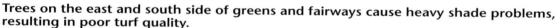

**Trees on the east and south side of greens and fairways cause heavy shade problems, resulting in poor turf quality.**

*Above*, trees can narrow down playing areas while preventing sun and air from getting through, leading to turf damage. *Below*, usually, the only effective solution is "tree management" (tree removal).

**Architect:** Tom Fazio, 1988    **Superintendent:** John Cunningham

# Black Diamond Ranch (Quarry)

## Lecanto, Florida

*Modern course profile*

Great golf courses are associated with powerful images. At Augusta National, it's Amen Corner. At St. Andrews, it's the Road Hole. For anyone who has played Black Diamond Ranch in Central Florida, it's undoubtedly the Quarry Holes.

Located in sleepy Lecanto, Florida, Black Diamond's Quarry Course features one of the most stunning string of holes in all of golf. Holes 13-17 play in and around two abandoned limestone quarries with vertical drops of up to 100 feet.

The five-hole odyssey starts with a jaw-dropping 183-yard par 3 across an 80-foot-deep chasm to a green perched (barely) on the far side. Two holes later, a deceptively short 371-yard par 4 doglegs left down into the other quarry. The putting surface at the 15th is framed by the quarry's towering canyon wall in the back and turquoise-blue water along the left.

And to think these quarries were once considered an eyesore by the previous landowner. When Black Diamond developer Stan Olsen purchased the abandoned 1,320-acre tract in 1982 the quarries weren't part of the original deal.

The reason? The seller thought the quarries, located 75 miles north of Tampa, might be a deal breaker, so they were excluded from the initial transaction. But while some saw "environmental savagery," Olsen saw "beauty" in the abandoned beasts and paid $60,000 for the quarries in a subsequent deal.

Now, in large part because of these quarries and the masterful touch of Tom Fazio, Black Diamond perennially is regarded as one of the top private golf communities in the country.

—*Scott Kauffman*

| | |
|---|---|
| Par | 72 |
| Yards | 7,159 |
| Slope | 133 |
| Rating | 74.8 |

**Golfweek Rating**

**7.31**

**Architect:** Tom Fazio, 1994     **Superintendent:** Travis Levings

# Karsten Creek Golf Club

## Stillwater, Oklahoma

Karsten Creek is scarcely what most people would imagine if they were to think about Central Oklahoma.

The course lies lightly upon gently rolling, wooded terrain just west of Stillwater. The 7,095-yard layout occupies a 960-acre site that leaves plenty of room for each hole corridor to feel secluded. Thick stands of native oak trees frame the holes, but architect Tom Fazio allowed plenty of room. The wide fairways lie naturally on the rugged terrain, and Fazio avoided constructing any artificial landforms.

Narrow, ribbon-like streams wind through the landscape. Plush zoysia grass carpets the fairways. Bentgrass graces the greens. Many of the fairways are expansive, but major errors more than likely will result in a challenging recovery because blackjack oaks and hackberry trees stand among thick undergrowth wide of the primary rough.

The first 15 holes wind through the woods and feature significant elevation changes. The final three holes emerge from the trees and surround Lake Louise, a 110-acre lake named after the wife of Ping founder Karsten Solheim. The course, by the way, bears his name because Solheim made a major financial contribution that got construction rolling. The course serves as the home facility for Oklahoma State University's golf teams.

The 20,000 square foot clubhouse is reminiscent of a mountain lodge. Amenities include a meeting room, outdoor patio and a full-service restaurant overlooking the 18th green. Visitors desiring an overnight visit also can rent one of six new apartments nearby. Not bad for a daily-fee course.

—*Bradley S. Klein*

| | |
|---|---|
| **Par** | 72 |
| **Yards** | 7,095 |
| **Slope** | 142 |
| **Rating** | 74.8 |

**Golfweek Rating**
7.22

# Desert Forest Golf Club

## Carefree, Arizona

**ModernCourseFeature**

### Links Golf in the Sonoran Foothills

*By Bradley S. Klein*

Desert Forest Golf Club, 35 miles northeast of downtown Phoenix, is a pioneering example of minimalist golf course design in a climate scarcely suited to the game. Its stark features and raw, bony character are derived from the native terrain, soil, rock and scrubby vegetation of the surrounding Sonoran Desert country.

This was America's first great example of desert golf course design and surely the finest work created by the much underappreciated Robert "Red" Lawrence" (1893-1976). There was no earth movement undertaken when the course was built in the early 1960s. Modest budget considerations forbade it, and it was Lawrence's design intent to lay the golf holes softly on the already well-contoured land.

Among Desert Forest's many unique aspects is the absence of any fairway bunkering—though the keen observer will note during a round the dominating role that one big "bunker"—the desert floor—plays on every tee shot. In an era when other desert courses have become lush, green oases, Desert Forest remains true to its design heritage with a firm, fast, Bermuda-grass turf cover that does not get overseeded in winter. The result is tawny, links-style playing surface perfectly suited to highlight the ground game.

A round here has the feel of an encounter very much "on the edge of doom," as if ice skating along a precipice. The fairways look generously wide but play narrow because they tend to be domed so that the golf ball runs off on either side into native desert scrub. Much strategy is created simply by alignment of the teeing grounds on the inside of the dogleg, making it extremely hard to hold the ball in the fairway because

| Par | 72 |
|---|---|
| Yards | 7,035 |
| Slope | 149 |
| Rating | 73.9 |

***Golfweek* Rating**
7.22

tee shots are either drawing into the left rough or angling through the far turn into the right rough.

This is very much an old-fashioned private golf club. The modest one-story clubhouse doesn't host evening social functions. Members sidle up to stools at the sunken bar of the lodge-like main room, where they have a dugout-level view of the golf course. Golf professional Doug MacDonald, club manager Scott Cromer and course superintendent Trevor Monreal all share a vision with the membership to keep Desert Forest a low-key throwback to the game in its traditional mode.

## America's Best: Rater's Notebook

### 1. Ease and intimacy of routing: 10
Easy access from green to next tee, thanks to a simple double loop of returning nines, with each side heading up to the far, higher end of the golf course and then gracefully returning to the clubhouse.

### 2. Quality of feature shaping: 6
Lovely native rolls to the fairways, with perched-up greens surrounded by deep, bathtub-like greenside bunkers and occasionally steep fallaway surrounds that leave delicate chips for recovery. The only variance from classical form is that the tees are more freeform than square.

### 3. Natural setting and overall land plan: 10
Here is a clear example of sport taking place amidst rather than against nature. Whatever peripheral housing there is remains distant and unobtrusive. Desert flora lightly frames every hole, and the views to the west, with Black Mountain providing the backdrop, are especially powerful. There is no better course in the Phoenix-Scottsdale area to play as late afternoon shadows stretch across the grounds.

### 4. Interest of greens and surrounding contours: 9
The surfaces appear tipped from back to front and yet fall off in subtle ways throughout, including to the rear. Modest entrances up front are available for carefully placed run-up shots, but recovery from around and beyond these 5,000 square-foot surfaces is delicate indeed, especially with the Seaside bentgrass rolling at 11-12 on the Stimpmeter.

### 5. Variety and memorability of par 3s: 5
Good variety of clubs required. The greens are all tightly protected, with more variance in terms of elevation change than in scorecard yardage. The uphill 191-yard 12th looks like there's nothing to hit to.

### 6. Variety and memorability of par 4s: 7
Crumpled fairways are hard to hold off the tee and never seem to leave a level lie. Good variability on playing length, especially with 453-yard 5th and 446-yard 13th playing uphill and requiring tee shots that draw slightly. Downhill 369-yard 14th, by contrast, calls for delicacy all the way, especially the short-iron/wedge approach to a tiny green squeezed all around by bunkers.

### 7. Variety and memorability of par 5s: 7
A native wash or barranca was a central element of the original par 5s, though in some areas it has been turfed over and taken out of play. It remains the major strategic element on the double-fairway 528-yard 7th hole, surely among the great true option holes in modern course design.

| Hole | 1 | 2 | 3 | 4 | 5 | 6 | 7 | 8 | 9 | Out | Card of the Course |
|---|---|---|---|---|---|---|---|---|---|---|---|
| Yardage | 375 | 428 | 168 | 394 | 453 | 369 | 534 | 206 | 501 | 3,446 | |
| Par | 4 | 4 | 3 | 4 | 4 | 4 | 5 | 3 | 5 | 36 | |

| Hole | 10 | 11 | 12 | 13 | 14 | 15 | 16 | 17 | 18 | In | Total |
|---|---|---|---|---|---|---|---|---|---|---|---|
| Yardage | 393 | 581 | 191 | 446 | 369 | 410 | 523 | 212 | 464 | 3,589 | 7,035 |
| Par | 4 | 5 | 3 | 4 | 4 | 4 | 5 | 3 | 4 | 36 | 72 |

## 8. Basic quality of conditioning: 7

Desert Forest sports quick greens, firm, fast Bermuda-grass fairways and thick, mid-irp. 134: Trees on the east and south side of greens and fairways cause heavy shade problems, resulting in poor turf quality.

## 9. Landscape and tree management: 8

Recent tree management program has reduced incursion of mesquite, palo verdes and pine trees and thinned out low-lying stands of smaller, prickly pear cactus that had spread. Remaining native saguaros and barrel cacti are stark reminders of the land's forbidding character.

## 10. "Walk in the park" test: 9

No cart paths; easily walked; a clubhouse that looks and feels like a piece of Western lore and a ground game sensibility without lakes, beverage carts, heroic carries or razzmatazz.

**Overall vote by *Golfweek* course raters: 7.22**

**Architect:** Pete Dye, 1981  **Superintendent:** Ashley Davis, CGCS

# Long Cove Golf Club

## Hilton Head Island, South Carolina

*Modern* course profile

| Par | 71 |
|---|---|
| Yards | 7,026 |
| Slope | 142 |
| Rating | 74.8 |

**Golfweek Rating**

**7.17**

Long Cove was the first course Pete Dye did in the aftermath of the controversy over TPC at Sawgrass (Stadium Course). He and his wife, Alice Dye, took great pains to make sure this one was playable for all golfers—an especially important consideration since it was the focal point of a high-end residential development and private club in the middle of the island.

For all his emphasis upon earth moving, Dye's best work is when he cuts features into the ground rather than piling them up. That stark, linear carved-out look makes the opening hole—a modest par-4 dogleg right around a pond—such an immense site. At Long Cove, Dye works angles brilliantly, always giving you a look at the target along the side of the hole that's closest to the dominant hazard and then asking you to play away.

At Long Cove, the one time Dye built up the playing surface is with the last few holes on the front nine, where he mounded a half-mile stretch to block out a busy local road.

Typical of Dye, the par 3s here are strong and varied. The 233-yard eighth is played to a steeply sloped, vaulted green, whereas the 163-yard 13th, across an inlet of marsh, plays to a dead-flat putting surface. Long Cove has a bit of unevenness to it. The 317-yard par-4 fifth is overly defended with a mid-fairway mound because Dye often gets nervous about such short par 4s. The green at the 590-yard, par-5 15th and the fairway shaping on the par-4 18th also are uncharacteristically busy. But such occasional over-reaching is the price one pays in the search for interesting golf holes. At Long Cove, the strengths carry the day by a long shot.

—*Bradley S. Klein*

# Greens Chairmen
## Type A and Type B

**By Bradley S. Klein**

There are two kinds of green committee chairmen. We'll call them "Type A" and "Type B." Both mean well. Both take their volunteer posts seriously. Both spend a lot of time with the superintendent and the course.

For all their input, however, they are worlds apart in terms of impact and legacy.

When Type A leaves office, everyone is relieved. When Type B's tenure is over, the course and its personnel are in better shape. Type A is an aggressive meddler. Type B, a steward of the game. Type A is usually a good golfer and has contempt for those who aren't. He—it's always a "he"—is well traveled, sees the top-rated courses in the country and is convinced that his home course is to neighboring clubs. In short, Type A sees himself as a hero.

He also fancies himself a monument builder. So he plants conifers. Moves bunkers. Tinkers with playing surfaces. Installs fountains. Removes evidence of the previous green chairman's meddling by shifting bunker styles and bulldozing ponds. "I've been here 25 years," one Mid-Atlantic superintendent told me. "We have exactly as many bunker styles as I've had green chairmen. I can go out there and identify each one. Flashed-up sand. Flat sand. Vertical grassed walls. Revetted sod bunkers. You name it, we have it."

This veteran greenkeeper survives by going along with the least offensive suggestions of

# "Type A is an aggressive meddler. Type B, a steward of the game."

(or should be) in equally fine shape. He's also convinced that his Herculean efforts alone are what keep the facility from total collapse. If he weren't out there every day peering over his greenkeeper's shoulder, the turf would die, the drainage lines would collapse, the club's design integrity would disappear and golfers would flock successive green chairmen while ignoring their more grandiose and costly projects. So the course lurches from one chair to the next, devoid of leadership, wracked by inconsistency, leaving the members cowering in a corner of the meeting room awaiting the passage of time.

Type A is a turf expert. He greets the maintenance crew each morning with his Stimpmeter in hand. He has every sprinkler head marked to identify yardage to the front, middle and back of greens. He has a vast library of books on architecture—some of which he has actually removed from their plastic wrappers. He is best buddies with "Jack" and "Greg." He spends his lunches at the club holding court. He tells the superintendent how to do his job. And then he appoints his successor, invariably from among his small circle of friends, even if the fellow has never before served on the green committee.

Type B is interested in golf but doesn't pose as an expert. Instead of dictating state-of-the-art techniques to the greenkeeper, he'll communicate what fellow members would like to see in terms of green speeds and course conditions, then ask two crucial questions: Are such conditions reasonable to expect of the golf course as it exists? And what level of budget, staffing and equipment does the superintendent need to get the job done? Instead of dictating, Type B listens. Instead of harassing the superintendent, Type B collaborates as the greenkeeper's advocate when it comes to presenting budget priorities to club officials.

Type B travels, but to a wide range of facilities, both low budget and high. He—or she—looks at restoration projects, attends regional and national seminars, and makes a point to stay informed and learn who the experts in the field are. When Type B has questions, consultants are contacted.

Clubs led by Type Bs have an annual green committee meeting in the maintenance building. The pro and the superintendent get along well. The members know the strengths and limits of their club and don't overreach by trying to convert their modest, family-oriented country club into a world-class championship venue. Instead of lurching from one project to the next, the club engages in long-term master planning. Rather than members discovering the day after the golf season closes that they've been tagged with a five-digit assessment, golfers get to attend informational meetings and vote on any major changes in fees, budgets or construction projects. Committees promote from within, so those who haven't served for several years can't wind up as chairman.

The differences in style between the two types of green chairmen are clear. The largely negative reputation acquired (and deserved) by Type As has led to a neglect of the proper way in which the job can be done. Type Bs, in their unassuming way, recognize the importance of their roles. They don't place themselves ahead of the course and they don't let personalities determine policy outcomes.

> ## "Type As have led to a neglect of the proper way in which the job can be done. Type Bs, in their unassuming way, recognize the importance of their roles."

**Architects:** Robert Trent Jones Sr., 1962 & 1977 • Rees Jones, 1989 & 1996    **Superintendent:** James J. Nicol, CGCS

# Hazeltine National Golf Club

## Chaska, Minnesota

*Modern course profile*

Hazeltine National, the brainchild of former U.S. Golf Association president Totton P. Heffelfinger, was conceived with one purpose in mind: to hold major golf championships. It always has been something of a work in progress, with tweaks by Robert Trent Jones Sr. before and after the 1970 U.S. Open—during which Dave Hill uttered his famous assessment: "They ruined a good farm when they built this course"—and further adjustments by Rees Jones for the 1991 Open and 2002 PGA Championship. Despite an initial look of immaturity, Hazeltine has evolved into an elegant parkland layout that has played host to five other USGA events, including U.S. Women's Opens in 1966 and 1977. Hazeltine also is the scheduled venue for the 2009 PGA Championship and the 2016 Ryder Cup Matches.

Hazeltine flexes its muscle with four lengthy par 5s. The shortest of the bunch—the 542-yard seventh with a third shot over water—may well be the trickiest. The 400-yard, par-4 16th is no picnic, with a narrow landing area flanked by a stream and woods, and an approach to a narrow peninsula green that juts into Lake Hazeltine.

"Because of its length, Hazeltine has a reputation of being a brute and a heavyweight, but a lot of yardage is on the par 5s," says Mike Schultz, the club's head professional. "I wouldn't call it a long hitter's course. It's more like Muhammad Ali—finesse and stuff. It's not a big bomber like Joe Frazier."

—*Dave Seanor*

| | |
|---|---|
| **Par** | 72 |
| **Yards** | 7,360 |
| **Slope** | 139 |
| **Rating** | 75.6 |
| **Golfweek Rating** | 7.15 |

# Calusa Pines Golf Club

## Naples, Florida

Western Florida isn't exactly known for dramatic landforms. So it's surprising—and interesting—to stumble upon a golf course in Naples with 50 feet of elevation change.

Calusa Pines brings together bold, beautiful features in a playful, almost theatrical manner. Four vast lakes were dug out, with the excavated dirt utilized to enhance the massive dunes that frame several of the holes. There are mature pines everywhere, plus 40 acres of sandy waste areas interspersed—much of it in lieu of traditional rough. The result is a sharply honed set of images involving finely maintained Tifeagle Bermuda-grass greens, TifSport tees and fairways juxtaposed against diverse textures of plant material, water and sand. The visual impact is not compromised by any real estate. At this private club, golf rules and everything else is secondary.

Golfers are tested at every point—though there's also plenty of room to play safe. Big hitters might be tempted to have a go at the green at the 300-yard, par-4 8th hole, thereby forgoing a fairly open layup shot. If they miss the drive a tad left, however, they face an awkward uphill second shot from a waste bunker to a plateau putting surface.

Water is in play on 10 holes, yet the shots all involve lateral or diagonal hazards rather than anxiety-provoking forced carries. That's the mark of an intelligent golf course; the extent of trouble here depends upon your ability to tolerate self-imposed risks. Another plus, especially compared to most Florida courses, is that the course is readily walkable, with greens close to tees and caddies always available.

—*Bradley S. Klein*

| | |
|---|---|
| **Par** | 72 |
| **Yards** | 7,198 |
| **Slope** | 140 |
| **Rating** | 74.9 |

***Golfweek* Rating**

**7.13**

**Architect:** Jack Nicklaus, 2000    **Superintendent:** Dale Engman

# Mayacama Golf Club

## Santa Rosa, California

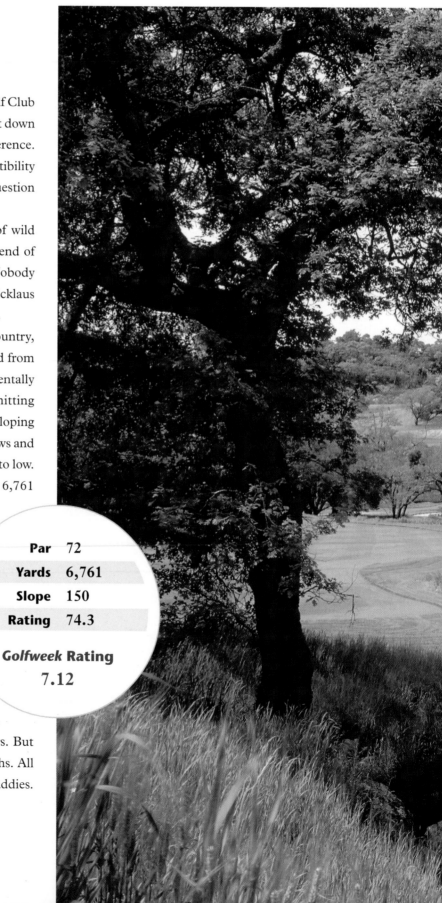

### Nature Intertwines at Mayacama

*By Bradley S. Klein*

During the opening day fete of Mayacama Golf Club in August 2000, course designer Jack Nicklaus sat down with the local and national media for a news conference. A question arose about the environmental compatibility of the layout with the native land—a fair enough question on a closely regulated site laced with wetlands.

Just as Nicklaus started to respond, a flock of wild turkeys appeared about 250 yards away at the far end of the practice range and waddled across the field. Nobody missed the power of the image. It said more than Nicklaus ever could about the coexistence of golf and nature.

Out here in the heart of Napa-Sonoma wine country, 60 miles north of San Francisco and 25 miles inland from the Pacific Ocean, developers have to be environmentally mindful or their projects won't survive the permitting process. The Mayacama site occupies 675 acres of sloping land. Oak stands are interspersed with grassy meadows and wetlands on land that falls 150 feet from high point to low. The focus of the land plan is a par-72 golf course, 6,761 yards from the back tees, 6,156 from the middle and a very forgiving 4,713 from the front markers. The course has five par 5s, five par 3s and eight par 4s and plays longer than the indicated yardage because many of the landing areas are graded into upslopes.

The land plan also calls for 31 home sites (one acre-plus each) and another cluster of 50 modest "casitas" intended for short-stay rental. The 37,000 square-foot Tuscan-style clubhouse includes an underground vault with 25 wine lockers for vintner members. But this is a golf club. There are no paved cart paths. All play proceeds in the company of uniformed caddies. Membership is very private.

| | |
|---|---|
| **Par** | 72 |
| **Yards** | 6,761 |
| **Slope** | 150 |
| **Rating** | 74.3 |

**Golfweek Rating**

7.12

## *America's Best: Rater's Notebook*

### 1. Ease and intimacy of routing: 7

Returning nines, both of them huge counterclockwise loops. There are only a few drawbacks—a road crossing and two awkward hikes, one of them an uphill slog from the 12th green. Par 3s bridge the most severely sloping ground. Forced carries off the tee are manageable. Three greens (holes 10, 13, and 15) are perched over deep fall-offs and leave no bailout option.

### 2. Quality of feature shaping: 6

Fairway features are tied in well to native grades and slopes; greens tend to be popped up and subject to a modest abruptness in their relationship to chipping areas and native terrain.

### 3. Natural setting and overall land plan: 8

Golf is juxtaposed dramatically against a background of rugged Mayacamas Mountains and foreground of lower profile woodlands and grassy meadows. Plans call for all housing and building development to be inconspicuous and deep in the woods.

### 4. Interest of greens and surrounding contours: 6

Good contour, transitions within putting surfaces; some chipping areas on the sides and behind are a bit too self-consciously shaped and stand out more than they should.

### 5. Variety and memorability of par 3s: 6

Green settings are diverse even if club selection varies little. During inaugural round, Nicklaus hit three 5-irons and two 6-irons. Reverse-Redan 11th is compelling, as is the fall-away green on 14.

### 6. Variety and memorability of par 4s: 7

Good mix of straight, left-to-right and right-to-left. No. 8 hole requires real shotmaking; too bad environmental constraints forced 16th to be (temporarily) shortened so that there's no real landing area.

### 7. Variety and memorability of par 5s: 8

All five par 5s present strong strategic options, including interesting second-shot demands—a rarity in par 5s today. Green on 15 is too thin from front to back and very unreceptive.

### 8. Basic quality of conditioning: 8

Sand capping to a depth of six inches on all the fairways provides firm base for quality turfgrass. Superintendent Dale Engman and crew preside over impeccably groomed bentgrass greens.

### 9. Landscape and tree management: 7

Two dozen live oaks were transplanted during clearing and construction, at a cost of up to $25,000 apiece. The occasional freestanding oak in the line of play is workable because of strategic options. The result is a mature-looking course, though understory is dense and impenetrable and landing areas occasionally get very pinched.

### 10. "Walk in the park" test: 8

A bracing walk at times, attractive to the senses, with the best part the scenic framing of many of the holes. A few long walks detract, however.

**Overall vote by *Golfweek* course raters: 7.12**

| Hole | 1 | 2 | 3 | 4 | 5 | 6 | 7 | 8 | 9 | Out | Card of the Course |
|---|---|---|---|---|---|---|---|---|---|---|---|
| Yardage | 434 | 525 | 178 | 501 | 188 | 420 | 320 | 411 | 568 | 3,565 | |
| Par | 4 | 5 | 3 | 5 | 3 | 4 | 4 | 4 | 5 | 37 | |
| Hole | 10 | 11 | 12 | 13 | 14 | 15 | 16 | 17 | 18 | In | Total |
| Yardage | 4397 | 205 | 441 | 404 | 159 | 537 | 298 | 196 | 559 | 3,196 | 6,761 |
| Par | 4 | 3 | 4 | 4 | 3 | 5 | 4 | 3 | 5 | 35 | 72 |

***Architect:*** Dick Wilson, 1964     ***Superintendent:*** Kenneth Lapp

# Cog Hill
# Golf Club (Dubsdread No. 4)
## Lemont, Illinois

| Par | 72 |
|---|---|
| **Yards** | **6,940** |
| **Slope** | **142** |
| **Rating** | **75.4** |

**Golfweek Rating**

**7.12**

Home of the Western Open since 1991, Cog Hill's aptly named Dubsdread is one of the favorite PGA Tour courses among professionals. The late Joe Jemsek, Cog Hill's owner, had it built as the gem of his 72-hole public complex, and it as served as a forerunner of high-end daily-fee tracks.

For the amateur, Dubsdread can be a brute. It is long and challenging, but also straightforward. Large oak trees line most fairways, and the greens are large, undulating, and well bunkered, with many of them cloverleaf-shaped. It's essential that someone be a good bunker player to score well here.

Jemsek used to go out on the course and give patrons this advice: When you are in between clubs, go with more club because the trouble is in the front of the green on most holes. He didn't mention there also is trouble on the sides.

The back nine is laid out alongside hills instead of from ridge to ridge. The guts of the course, some might say, start at the par-3 12th, played downhill to a perched green.

Dubsdread also was host to the 1997 U.S. Amateur, won by Matt Kuchar. In a city legendary for the quality of its public-access courses, Dubsdread set the standard and continues to lead the pack.

—***Jeff Rude***

*Architect:* Jim Engh, 1997    *Superintendent:* Dave Hare

# The Sanctuary

## Sedalia, Colorado

When Dave Liniger, co-founder and chairman of real estate giant RE/MAX, was seeking to build his dream course, The Sanctuary, in Sedalia, Colorado, he brought in seven big-name architects to a 222-acre site in Castle Rock. The land offered stunning vistas of the Rocky Mountains, along with 800 feet of elevation change from low point (6,000 feet above sea level) to high. Two designers pronounced the course unbuildable. Five others said it would be extraordinarily expensive.

Not Jim Engh, whom Liniger had earlier befriended when they were paired together in a golf outing. Liniger said they spent many hours together in Engh's office talking over the craft. Liniger especially was intrigued by the precision of the architect's line drawings. He then took Engh out on a daylong walk of the steep, rocky site and at the end of their trek offered him the job. Engh not only designed every line and every feature of the site but also oversaw construction.

The problem on any such site is making the uphill terrain work. Engh did it by incorporating many of the uphill climbs into the land between greens and the next tee. Fourteen holes play downhill or level; the other four play uphill, and Engh made these paths work by creating plateaus that would hold the ball and prevent it from backing up too far. For dramatic effect, Engh placed the first tee on a virtual pedestal looking out onto the great Western frontier, with a 185-foot vertical drop to the fairway on a 604-yard, par-5 hole.

Liniger built The Sanctuary as a private enclave for his friends and as a venue to host charity golf tournaments. It offers "rock 'em, sock 'em" imagery and some sharply etched strategic choices for landing areas. Throw in a few waterfalls (at the owner's insistence) and the distant backdrop of the Rocky Mountains and you have a course ranked No. 37 on the Modern list.

—*Bradley S. Klein*

| Par | 72 |
|---|---|
| Yards | 7,033 |
| Slope | 142 |
| Rating | 72.3 |

*Golfweek* Rating

7.12

**Architects:** Tom Weiskopf & Jay Morrish, 1988    **Superintendent:** Andrew J. Annan, CGCS

*Modern* course profile

# Forest Highlands Golf Club (Canyon)

## Flagstaff, Arizona

So much for rules of routing and hole sequence. Here's a golf course with only four holes in the 400- to 499-yard range. It has five par 5s, three of them more than 600 yards. And it has six par 3s, all of them compressed into an 11-hole stretch in the middle of the round and all of them on even-numbered holes—4, 6, 8, 10, 12, 14.

At Forest Highlands Golf Club's Canyon Course, you don't notice oddities because your mind and eyes are so taken in by the golf holes and the scenery. Being 7,000 feet above sea level in Northern Arizona's San Francisco Peaks has an effect on you, especially when you're playing through a Ponderosa pine forest where the trees are more than 100 feet tall. Everything is on a big scale—the bunkers (only 41 of them), the split fairway options, the bentgrass greens and the setbacks to unobtrusive private residences.

The air is crystal-clear here—ideal for golf in a season that runs from early May through October. The humidity is usually in the single digits, temperature swings of 40-50 degrees in a playing day are commonplace, and only 80 days per year are frost-free. At Forest Highlands, you learn to dress in layers and to slather on plenty of sunblock. You also learn how good Tom Weiskopf and Jay Morrish were at the zenith of their design partnership.

—*Bradley S. Klein*

| | |
|---|---|
| **Par** | 71 |
| **Yards** | 7,051 |
| **Slope** | 134 |
| **Rating** | 73.1 |

**Golfweek Rating**
**7.09**

**Architect:** Tom Fazio, 1995    **Superintendent:** Mark Sundeen

# Estancia

## Scottsdale, Arizona

| Par | 72 |
|---|---|
| Yards | 7,146 |
| Slope | 137 |
| Rating | 73.7 |

***Golfweek* Rating**

**7.05**

In Scottsdale, Arizona, stunning golf locales are as plentiful as cacti and massive umber-colored boulders. So when something comes along recently and makes an impression as strong as Estancia has, you know you're onto something special. Here, Tom Fazio routed a course on this 640-acre property prior to the release of home sites. That means he had control of the land plan—no small advantage to a designer looking to maximize golf and avoid getting squeezed by residential development.

The course sits on rolling, high desert terrain on the northern slope of Pinnacle Peak, with the holes coiling around both the northern and southern flank of the famed landmark.

Almost every tee shot starts from an elevated position at Estancia. Seldom will players encounter the slender ribbon of fairway typical of Arizona layouts, where the desert looms intrusively on both sides. Here the fairways are cut generously, with wide expanses of rough flanking the short grass. While tee ball targets can be up to 90 yards wide, the approach shots are far less forgiving. A couple of streams meander the property and demand attention. Bentgrass greens are on the small side and undulating, many with three separate levels.

Perhaps the most memorable hole is also the smallest. The par-3 11th, only 137 yards, flows between massive boulders. The tee shot features a panorama that encompasses seven holes on the property. The view quickly is transformed into a desperate search for the flag when the day's hole placement is way left, tucked behind the largest rock outcropping.

Estancia is geared for golf. All else is secondary.

—***Bradley S. Klein***

**Architects:** W. Chandler Egan, 1928 • Robert Trent Jones Sr., 1967    **Superintendent:** Chris Gaughan

# Eugene Country Club

## Eugene, Oregon

*Modern course profile*

Eugene Country Club is the only one of *Golfweek*'s top Modern courses that dates to the Classical courses period. How can it straddle both categories? And why is it considered Modern?

The answer is simple. Eugene CC originally was designed by H. Chandler Egan and opened in 1928. Then, in 1967, Robert Trent Jones performed a total renovation, bumping it into the Modern group.

This was no ordinary makeover. Jones surprised the membership by proposing that he preserve all of the corridors of the Egan layout but simply reverse the direction they played. The new first tee would be built in the area of the old No. 18 green, the new first green would be near the old 18th tee, and so forth. This suggestion accomplished something near and dear to the hearts of club members: the course was never closed during the

Jones redesign. New greens and tees were built alongside existing greens and tees, and golfers continued to play the original course until the new one was ready.

Not wanting to lose members or revenue, officers of the club endorsed the $433,000 plan ($386,000 for the course, $47,000 for the golf shop and parking lot). After the renovation, monthly dues soared, from $8 to $33.

The fairways mostly were untouched by Jones, and virtually no trees had to be removed. Average green size was increased from about 3,000 square feet to 6,500 square feet.

Today, the club is firmly entrenched in the U.S. Golf Association rotation, having hosted three national championships (1964 U.S. Junior won by Johnny Miller, 1993 U.S. Mid-Amateur won by Jeff Thomas and 2002 U.S. Women's Mid-Amateur won by Kathy Hartwiger).

*—James Achenbach*

| Par | 72 |
|-----|-----|
| Yards | 6,854 |
| Slope | 139 |
| Rating | 73.7 |

**Golfweek Rating**

**7.04**

# First-Rate Fazio

## Veteran Architect Has Nine Original Layouts on the Modern List

### By John Steinbreder

Tom Fazio didn't waste a lot of time getting into the design business. The Philadelphia native was only 17 when he started helping his Uncle George design courses in 1962. Since then, Fazio, now 58 years old, has built a remarkable portfolio. All told, 150 layouts bear his name, including nine original designs among our top-50 Modern courses.

While he is clearly proud of what he has achieved, the thought of all those projects lumped together makes him cringe.

"It's a lot of work, and an awful lot of years," he says. "It really makes me sound very old."

It also makes him sound successful. And why shouldn't it, with standouts on the roster such as Shadow Creek Golf Club in North Las Vegas, Nevada (No. 6), Wade Hampton Club in Cashiers, North Carolina (No. 15), Dallas National Golf Club in Dallas, Texas (No. 17), World Woods Golf Club's Pine Barrons Course in Brooksville, Florida (No. 23), the Quarry Course at Black Diamond Ranch in Lecanto, Florida (No. 29), Karsten Creek Golf Club in Stillwater, Oklahoma (No. 30), Estancia in Scottsdale, Arizona (No. 39), Galloway National Golf Club in Galloway Township, New Jersey (No. 42) and Victoria Hills Golf Club in Newburgh, Indiana (No. 45). That does not take into account all the renovation work he has done, including low-profile tweaking of Augusta National Golf Club and Winged Foot Golf Club. Fazio also has won a slew of industry honors, including the prestigious Old Tom Morris Award presented by the Golf Course Superintendents Association of America.

He is not without his controversies. Some critics claim that Fazio spreads himself too thin as an architect. Others chide him for catering mostly to high-profile projects and building courses many golfers cannot afford to play.

He's certainly not one to shy away from criticism, as the following interview, conducted by senior writer John Steinbreder, attests.

*Golfweek: How much time do you personally spend on a project?*

**Fazio:** I only do one thing, and that is design golf courses. And I spend a lot of time on it because I have always had a very strong work ethic and structure. I have been working most of my life, and up until the time I got married I worked seven days a week. My uncle was among those who taught me about hard work, and it took me a while after I got married to get over the guilty feelings I had when I was not working on a Saturday or Sunday. For the last 20 years, I'd say I have worked five days a week on average. But I love to stay in the office until 7 p.m. or so on those days, because I love what I do so much. To me, it is not really hard, and it is not really work.

As for how much time I spend on each project, I do not have a certain amount set aside. It all really depends on the stage of things and when they're approved and what needs to be done. There is never an automatic time I have to give to any one.

Generally speaking, I will go as much as three times a month to an individual project and check on things. One of my senior staff members will probably go once a week, and one of our design associates will be there four or five days a week to work with the contractor on a daily basis. Our involvement is quite significant.

My business is my life, and I still remember every golf hole I ever did. I can go through every one of my courses hole by hole and know exactly how they were done. I remember the years of my life by the golf courses I was doing during those times.

***Golfweek:*** *How big a staff do you have?*

**Fazio:** I have 10 senior design associates. The newest one of those has been with me for 12 years, and the oldest, 27 years. Then I have 12 additional younger people we call design associates. Our additional support staff comes to about 10, and I am the only one who is involved in all the projects.

***Golfweek:*** *How many offices?*

**Fazio:** Three. The original one was in Jupiter, Florida, and when my wife and I moved to North Carolina 18 years ago, we opened a new one there in Hendersonville. Later on, we went to Scottsdale, Arizona, which is where our third office is today.

***Golfweek:*** *What do you charge per course?*

**Fazio:** The price varies based on location, region and time. But, I would say that the general range of my fee is about $1 million per project.

***Golfweek:*** *Do you have a favorite course that you have designed?*

**Fazio:** Not really. There are so many of them I like, and I truly believe they are all of the highest quality. Plus, most of my clients are personal friends, and I don't want to get any of them upset by answering that question a certain way.

***Golfweek:*** *It sometimes appears that you are dismissive of classical course architects and their work. Is that so?*

**Fazio:** Being from the Northeast, I am a fan of a number of the older architects, like (A. W.) Tillinghast and Donald Ross. I also think Alister MacKenzie did wonderful work. I have seen a lot of old courses, and I love them because they show me all the things we can't do today.

***Golfweek:*** *What do you mean by that?*

**Fazio:** There is just a lot they did back then that would not be acceptable today from a quality standpoint. Like blind holes. You saw a lot of them on the older courses, but today those would not be acceptable to many people. You have places like Cypress Point, which have two par 3s in a row and two par 5s in a row. Great course, right? But how would people building a golf course today like that? Probably not very many.

If you go to different older courses, you often have several good holes, several medium holes and several average holes. But if you have several average holes in this current environment, you could lose a lot. Architects get grief about one weak hole, and something like that can be taken as a great failure. People are so highly critical today, and it's a problem.

That's one reason why we had in the 1980s what I call the decade of bad courses. There was so much criticism that designers went overboard trying to make every hole an 18th hole, every hole a difficult hole, as if they were trying to impress someone.

Honestly, I think the out-and-out quality of the modern courses is more consistent. It has to be because of the scrutiny and the competition. I believe there is a lot to learn from the classic architects, but we need to take that, use modern technology and know-how, and bring it to the future.

***Golfweek:*** *Why are so many of your courses high-end?*

**Fazio:** Mostly because I strive to do the best possible golf course every time. As an architect, I also get calls from people who want to do something special, who want to do something better than someone else I worked for, and I can't help but jump all over opportunities like those. In addition, there are lots of people who design courses where golf is the second, third, or maybe even fourth priority. But those are places I do not want to go.

**Golfweek:** *Some people say you should give something back to golf by doing some less upscale courses.*

**Fazio:** I don't know about that. I work very hard on some charities in the area where I live, and it's a very important part of my life. I've been donating a lot of time for them and raising a lot of money for things like the Boys & Girls Club of Hendersonville and East Flat Rock, so I feel that I am doing something positive in that regard, that I am giving something back, though it may not all be to golf.

I have done some public courses, but I haven't done any recently because I haven't found the right opportunity. I suppose I could create a division within my company to do those, but in many ways I feel I would just be taking work away from other architects who need those sorts of projects to get their start in the game and make their mark. I mean, should Frank Lloyd Wright have done government housing?

**Golfweek:** *You have said before that the land on which you build a course doesn't really matter, that you can build a course anywhere. How so?*

**Fazio:** I think for the modern era that is true because we can do so much ourselves. I would not have said that was the case prior to the 1980s, but I think my work at Shadow Creek proved it. Also, if you have a good piece of land today, like what you have at Pebble Beach, or a place with nice streams, you probably would not be able to build there because of environmental concerns. But you can build your own creek, and you can build it exactly where you want it. Plus, the weakest pieces of land are less likely to create environmental permitting problems for you.

As far as I am concerned, nothing can stop us from building great golf courses. I could take the Mall of America, and all its parking lots, and there is no reason I could not build a great golf course on that spot.

## The Tom Fazio File

**Born:** Feb. 10, 1945
**Hometown:** Norristown, Penn.
**Residence:** Hendersonville, N.C.
**Family:** Wife, Sue; daughters, Jenon, Keegan and Onae; sons, Logan, Austin and Gavin.
**Occupation:** President and owner, Fazio Golf Course Designers Inc.
**Etc.:** Won the Old Tom Morris Award by the Golf Course Superintendents Association of America in 1996. Tom and Sue Fazio are active in the community and support many local charities, art and theater associations. The Fazios founded the Boys & Girls Club of Hendersonville in 1993 and the Boys & Girls Club of East Flat Rock in 1998.

**Architect:** Tom Doak, 1999    **Superintendent:** Steve Jotzat, CGCS

# Lost Dunes Golf Club

## Bridgman, Michigan

*Modern* course profile

At Lost Dunes, Tom Doak shows his emerging confidence. Without trying directly to copy famous holes, as he had in the past, he relies, instead, on evoking basic strategic principles and then letting fly with his own forms to fit the site.

That was no easy matter on an abandoned sand quarry that had a major highway splitting it down the middle, as well as environmentally sensitive wetlands and ponds. Just getting out and back to the clubhouse on adequate ground proved hard enough. Doak solved the problem with an inventive idea—head out to the first tee via a road crossing that gets it done with before the round starts. That way, you can warm up, walk over to the first tee, and play a round that fits comfortably.

As if the ground didn't have enough yaw and pitch, Doak made sure that putting would never be boring either.

Superintendent Steve Jotzat has his hands full making sure he keeps green speeds manageable given the strength of some of the contours. Buried elephants? The putting green at the 525-yard, par-5 fourth looks like a sound stage for *Wild Kingdom*. The beauty here is that such contours remain a challenge for everybody, regardless of how long (or short) they hit the ball. Doak, ever the classicist, knows that when it comes to protecting par, distance only goes so far, while the ground game lasts forever.

*—Bradley S. Klein*

| | |
|---|---|
| **Par** | 71 |
| **Yards** | 6,905 |
| **Slope** | 134 |
| **Rating** | 73.7 |

*Golfweek* **Rating**
7.03

# Galloway National Golf Club

## Galloway Township, New Jersey

Most golf courses in the Atlantic City area are flat. Galloway National's neighbor to the immediate south, for example, the Donald Ross-designed Bay Course at the Marriott Seaview Resort, has less than five feet of fall. At Galloway National, Tom Fazio had 40 feet of elevation to work with, which gave him a chance to work all sorts of rolls and sweeps into the layout. Its setting—on Reeds Bay, looking out to Brigantine Island—exposes the course to winds off the Atlantic Ocean only five miles to the east.

There's a pine barrens feel to the place, evident in the sandy scrub through which many of the holes are routed. At the 146-yard, par-3 second hole, Fazio takes golfers along a marshy inlet, then heads them back inland. The course returns dramatically to the shoreline at the 249-yard, par-3 17th. Here, the tee shot is oriented down a narrow chute of pine trees, with the hotels and casinos of downtown Atlantic City perched directly, if at a distance, behind the green.

—*Bradley S. Klein*

| Par | 71 |
| --- | --- |
| Yards | 6,901 |
| Slope | 142 |
| Rating | 73.8 |

*Golfweek* **Rating**
7.02

*Modern* course profile

**Architect:** Bobby Weed, 2000    **Superintendent:** Marc Eubanks

# Olde Farm Golf Club

## Bristol, Virginia

They do things differently at Olde Farm in the far western corner of Virginia. Some fancy private clubs have manned guardhouses, palatial clubhouses and extensive conference facilities. At Olde Farm, you drive over a cattle crossing, the Colonial-style clubhouse comes from a design by Thomas Jefferson, and the two outbuildings on the golf course are whitewashed barns, one of them an old tobacco-curing shed.

The golf course combines old-world charm with the latest agronomic advances. The tees, fairways and putting surfaces are tightly mowed L-93 bentgrass that's kept fast and firm. The bluegrass roughs are framed by unmaintained areas that include fine fescue and native grasses. Bobby Weed, true to his classical architecture commitments, revetted many of the bunkers and gave them a weepy, scratchy look. Then he sprinkled all sorts of rolls and cross-bunkers into the fairways to create multiple options on every full shot.

The 175 acres composing the course are ideal golf ground, with 75 feet of elevation change and a stream, called Sinking Creek, that weaves in and out of play on six holes. Throughout Olde Farm, Weed makes great use of diagonally arrayed hazards. He's especially good at bringing the creek into play on oblique angles that create all sorts of strategy. That's the strength of several par 4s, including the 322-yard eighth and the 453-yard 17th.

—*Bradley S. Klein*

| | |
|---|---|
| **Par** | 71 |
| **Yards** | 6,857 |
| **Slope** | 127 |
| **Rating** | 73.4 |

*Golfweek* **Rating**
**7.00**

# Princeville Golf Club (Prince)

## Kauai, Hawaii

Princeville Resort occupies a beautiful site on Kauai's north shore that stretches from the Pacific Ocean to the Hanalei Valley. The Prince Course sprawls over 390 acres, with some of the holes perched along coastal highlands, 150 feet above the shoreline. The genius of the layout is the way it incorporates diverse terrain, including a lava tube, a streambed, and dense stands of tropical vegetation, including guava and papaya trees.

The fairways are wide enough to accommodate the winds that often howl across the land. Strategic variety is ensured by holes that run along, up to and across the finger-like ravines that crease the site.

Perhaps the most dramatic scene to be found is on the 205-yard, par-3 seventh hole. The tee shot must carry over a densely vegetated ravine that ties into Anini Beach on the left. The hole is a good example of architect Robert Trent Jones Jr.'s sense of land, adventure and aesthetics. For years, he had the run of some dramatic sites in the American west to build on, including high desert plains and mountain valleys. At Princeville, Jones achieved something rare—making a steep site work well for shotmaking while enabling the land to express itself fully and naturally.

—*Bradley S. Klein*

| Par | 72 |
|---|---|
| Yards | 7,309 |
| Slope | 145 |
| Rating | 75.3 |

**Golfweek Rating**

**6.99**

**Architect:** Tom Fazio, 1999    **Superintendent:** Dale R. Minick, CGCS

# Victoria National Golf Club

## Newburgh, Indiana

Tom Fazio's talent for transforming landforms knows no bounds. That's evident at Victoria National, in an eastern suburb of Evansville, Indiana. There he took an abandoned strip mine and rehabilitated it into a stunning set of golf holes. Owner Terry Friedman has aspirations that the private club will one day be the site of a major national championship. After seeing how this tattered pile of open pits, deep trenches and mine tailings has become nationally ranked golf ground, anything is possible.

The par 3s in particular are daunting, with three of them calling for a forced carry over an isthmus of land to a target that looks as if it's suspended in marshy ooze. The front nine has a more open farmland feel. The back nine is decidedly more aggressive in tone and shaping. Forget abut bailout options; they've all been foreclosed.

Holes 14-15-16 compose an especially difficult sequence. The green at the tree-squeezed, 471-yard, par-4 14th is perched 20 feet above the fairway. The 548-yard, par-5 15th has a fairway that's shaped like a jitterbugging dinosaur. The only reprieve at the 208-yard, par-3 16th is that the hole plays downhill. The tiered putting surface offers no marginal land short, long, left or right. Other than that, it's a snap.

So what if the place plays hard? Victoria National has a swampy, misty, primordial look about it that is compelling from the first tee. There's nothing backward about the club or its conditioning, however. Even in a notoriously tough climate, the bentgrass tees, fairways and greens are kept in immaculate shape.

—*Bradley S. Klein*

| Par | 72 |
|---|---|
| Yards | 7,239 |
| Slope | 143 |
| Rating | 75.4 |

**Golfweek Rating**
**6.98**

# Pumpkin Ridge
# Golf Club (Witch Hollow)

## Cornelius, Oregon

| Par | 72 |
| --- | --- |
| Yards | 7,017 |
| Slope | 141 |
| Rating | 74.8 |

**Golfweek Rating**
**6.94**

When Pumpkin Ridge opened in 1991, it set a new standard for design, aesthetics and conditioning and raised expectations for a subsequent decade of what became an Oregon golf boom.

The setting helps, 22 miles west of Portland, on the edge of the Willamette Valley, with the Tualatin Hills to the south and the Coast Ridge to the west. The facility is actually a 36-hole project; in a unique undertaking, a daily-fee course (Ghost Creek) shares the 341-acre site with Witch Hollow, the private course. They have separate clubhouses and use the same 20-acre practice ground, though the tees are arrayed at each other 320 yards apart.

Witch Hollow makes lovely use of wetlands, mature native hardwoods and deep, classically inspired bunkers. In its short history the course has also seen some epic competitions. Tiger Woods won his last U.S. Amateur here in 1996. The next year, Alison Nicholas eked out a win over Nancy Lopez in the Women's Open. In 2003, underdog Hilary Lunke was the surprise winner of the Women's Open. The last two events both came down to 18th hole dramatics, but then so do most rounds at Pumpkin Ridge-Witch Hollow. The one sure bet at this 545-yard par-5—it calls for two forced carries over wetlands to a plateau green—is that between the tee and the green, a lot of money will change hands.

—*Bradley S. Klein*

*Modern course profile*

# Musgrove Mill Golf Club

## Clinton, South Carolina

Musgrove Mill Golf Club in rural Clinton, South Carolina , is one of those largely undiscovered gems that seem to be located in the middle of nowhere. Those who play Musgrove Mill for the first time often compare the course to revered Pine Valley Golf Club, which was the inspiration for this layout.

Musgrove, completed in 1992, is widely credited to the design firm of Arnold Palmer and Ed Seay, although most of the recognition should go to a small group of South Carolinians who loved golf and to one member of that founding group in particular—tax attorney Ken Tomlinson.

Tomlinson and friends, wrestling with a shortage of capital, unsuccessfully tried to interest designer Tom Fazio in Musgrove. Later, they persuaded Palmer and Seay to lend their names to the project, and Seay produced a routing plan.

That essentially was it for Palmer and Seay, as Tomlinson changed part of the routing plan, moved tees and greens, and finally supervised the building of the course. The total construction cost was a bargain-basement $2 million.

Highlights at Musgrove include some dramatic elevation changes, with several tees and greens located on promontories above the valley below. There is enough sand and wasteland to foster images of Pine Valley.

Tomlinson, for his part, went on to design and build another intriguing course, Tidewater Plantation in Cherry Grove Beach, South Carolina.

—*James Achenbach*

| | |
|---|---|
| **Par** | 72 |
| **Yards** | 6,933 |
| **Slope** | 144 |
| **Rating** | 74 |

**Golfweek Rating**
**6.92**

# Steering Clear of Wetlands

**By Lynn Henning**

Tom Weiskopf remembers tearing at his hair "and ultimately tearing up a course routing" in the mid-1990s while designing a handsome 18-hole layout at Shanty Creek Resort in Bellaire, in the heart of northern Michigan's tourist land.

Weiskopf was not happy that two holes on a particularly lovely back nine were about to be thwarted by a group of citizens dubbed Friends of the Cedar River.

There had been a grand idea on the designer's part. A fast-flowing, brush-embanked ribbon of water, the Cedar River, would be crossed twice as part of Weiskopf's 13th and 14th holes.

They would be signature holes all the way— daring, scenic, awesome. A nervy par 3 would be followed by a perfectly conceived short par 4.

One problem: The Friends of the Cedar River decided those holes would be built over their drowned bodies. An effort to nix Weiskopf's plan was mounted, one that Shanty Creek ultimately decided not to contest in the interests of diplomacy.

Weiskopf went back to work. His response today to the changes he was obliged to make, and to the design that now exists along a particularly distinctive stretch of the Cedar River course, is almost amusing.

"Best thing that ever happened," said Weiskopf, the great Tour player from decades past who now is almost solely focused on his Scottsdale, Arizona-based firm, Tom Weiskopf Golf Design.

"I actually believe, and I'm not saying this because I want to give it back to the environmentalists, but I know it turned out better this way than it would have with the original thought."

Not all anecdotes are as giddy when course design and the environment's needs crash head on.

And not all confrontations are the product of zealous pro-ecology, anti-golf interests clashing with course architects who never met a wetland they didn't want to drain or fill.

The issues are deep, without necessarily being divisive. Wetlands restrictions were long overdue in America, as nearly all fair-minded parties agree. The degree to which threatened species restrictions or wetlands preservation acts can make an impact on course design, however, can leave an architect wondering if common sense might ever triumph.

In the midst of a promising routing it also can leave a course architect all but crying that a for-the-ages golf hole is being thwarted by a few square yards of cattails. At the same time, architects acknowledge genuine wetlands are as much a treasure as a business reality.

"I think, in general, we are recognizing the values of well developed wetlands to the environment, and we didn't do that even 10 years ago," said Hurdzan/Fry Golf Design.

"But in the same way we can't paint all wetlands with the same brush. At least half the wetlands we've dealt with are simply wet areas, and really have no environmental value. I would say, without question, we have compromised many, many golf holes because of wetlands, and sometimes because of pitiful wetlands."

Hurdzan recalls a project not long ago where, smack-dab in the middle of a centerpiece hole, problems loomed. A tree had been dug from a hole that now stretched six feet across and had filled with water. Some wetlands plants had become rooted in the crater.

Environmental overseers wanted the "wetland" preserved. Hurdzan wanted a

associated with wetlands, and with the long carries they might require, have been reduced by the past decade's trend toward multiple tees.

In step with Hurdzan and most designers, Forrest and Hills try to put tees next to broad wetland areas. It is easier to hit a tee ball over a marshland than to negotiate that same wetland with an approach shot.

# "More than a designer's creative preferences can be at stake when designs and environmental rules bump heads."

reasonable interpretation of what he thought the area certainly was: a mud hole containing vegetation. Hurdzan won. The hole was built. An eminently better course was the result.

More than a designer's creative preferences can be at stake when designs and environmental rules bump heads. Playability issues—forced carries that can frustrate and penalize golfers, and speed-of-play hindrances that send golfers packing—also are part of the fight to balance good design with smart stewardship.

"Some courses I've seen in Florida are simply unplayable for higher handicap golfers, and that's not good for the game, nor, quite frankly, is it any fun," said Hurdzan, who tries to abide by two rules of thumb for forced carries: no more than 100 yards for men, no more than 60 yards for women.

Steve Forrest, one half of the Arthur Hills-Steve Forrest & Associates design firm from Toledo, Ohio, says many of the headaches once

Tom Doak knows all about wetlands and how they can change a layout. He winces every time someone mentions the 18th hole at High Pointe, his first major design project, in Williamsburg, Michigan, not far from Traverse City.

Doak was ready to wrap up a terrific finishing hole, a par 5 played around, or over, a lake. Wetlands regulations ended up forcing him to drastically change the tee shot. It remains a 5-wood drive from the tee, at most, and the ball must nestle into a tight landing area before the hole's strength and character emerge.

"We thought we'd be able to get an exciting finishing hole there, but we didn't get the wetlands flagged in the field until late in the process, and then they made us steer around an area we thought we'd be able to use," said Doak.

"It made for a tough second shot and a very frustrating hole. Since then, if I'm going to get anywhere near a wetland, I'll make sure I get it flagged in the field before we commit to any routing."

Doak notes the different problems posed by wetlands and streams. Wetlands are wider. They can be hyper-restrictive. Streams, on the other hand, often are an enhancer, which is what Doak, for the most part, found when he designed Stonewall in Elverson, Pennsylvania.

A stream on Stonewall's sixth hole creates a perfect driving hazard, and, because it is only six feet wide, some kind of recovery shot normally is possible.

"But back on the fifth hole, the same stream has a bunch of wetlands to either side," Doak said, "so if your tee shot falls short of the green, you can't drop within 50 yards. And then there is a bunch of wetland growth in your way for the provisional ball."

Double-edged swords abound when a designer tromps a tract of land or obsesses over a topographical map, trying to figure out what wetlands might allow him to do with a routing.

Weiskopf thinks back to his Cedar River experience and remembers how, the minute he quit fuming about those mandated changes to his early design, the more he saw options that resulted in a better trade-off.

The 13th hole now is a sensational 297-yard par 4 with a split fairway. The Cedar River's rushing waters can be heard in the background, a neat audio treat that meshes nicely with the back nine's ambience.

The 14th is a 163-yard par 3, and a dandy. Tee shots fall 80 feet to a green tucked against the riverbank.

Accepting the fact that laws and regulations are different than they were in Donald Ross's day would, in Weiskopf's view, be refreshing.

A stream—and its surrounding wetlands—proved to be a challenge for Tom Doak on the 5th and 6th holes at Stonewall.

"We tend to dwell too much on the past. We look back to holes we thought were really sensational that were built before all this wetlands policing came about," Weiskopf said, "and then we say, 'Gee whiz, if I could do this or that it would really be a fantastic hole.'

"We've got to let it go. I still believe some of the best golf courses built in the 20th century were built in the '90s, and had those earlier guys had the same constraints, the same wetlands to deal with, they'd do these courses today no differently.

"These are the rules. Challenge your imagination and your creativity. And come up with something you're very proud of."

ModernCourseFeature

# Quintero Golf and Country Club

## Peoria, Arizona

### Harnessing the Frontier

*By Bradley S. Klein*

How far out in the Sonoran Desert do you have to go to be a pioneer these days? With Quintero Golf Club, the answer is clear—40 miles northwest of downtown Phoenix, halfway on the road to Wickenburg. That's about as remote as Desert Forest Golf Club in Carefree, Arizona, was when that innovative tract opened in 1962, and now burgeoning development north of Scottsdale has caught up to it.

Quintero's owner and visionary, Gary McClung, is counting on the same thing happening to his property. He acquired a remote 820-acre former mining site in the middle of an area under the jurisdiction of the U.S. Bureau of Land and Mines. McClung then had to lay miles of internal roads, put up his own generators and run a pipeline 6 miles to tap into the Central Arizona Project for (recycled) irrigation water. Along the way, he hired Rees Jones and had the good sense to leave him and design associate Steve Weiser alone to do their work.

Build it and they will come? That's apparently the hope here, where plans include 283 home sites and another golf course, this one designed by Greg Norman, slated for the more rugged section of the property, to the northeast. For now, members have the run of a spectacular layout that manages to be walkable while playing in a gentle fashion despite some very stark landforms and 150 feet of elevation change on the golf holes.

Routing is the key to making any tough site work. Quintero was especially challenging because the area Jones had to work with left only three valley passes around five major hills, and one of those low areas was taken by the entrance road.

| | |
|---|---|
| **Par** | 72 |
| **Yards** | 7,190 |
| **Slope** | 145 |
| **Rating** | 75.1 |

**Golfweek** Rating
**6.91**

Rock abounded—quartz and red and black granite, as well as shale. But there also was much undisturbed native vegetation. Preserving the desert flora gave Quintero a surprisingly mature look when it opened. It helps that several groups of holes exist in their own little pockets of land—away from infrastructure and roads.

For now, Quintero exists very much on its own expansive world, which is exactly the appeal of the place. Given what the long-term land plan looks like, there's every reason to believe that subsequent housing will be kept isolated, in clusters and set back from the golf.

| Hole | 1 | 2 | 3 | 4 | 5 | 6 | 7 | 8 | 9 | Out | |
|---|---|---|---|---|---|---|---|---|---|---|---|
| Yardage | 388 | 571 | 406 | 460 | 374 | 219 | 431 | 586 | 212 | 3,647 | |
| Par | 4 | 5 | 4 | 4 | 4 | 3 | 4 | 5 | 3 | 36 | Card of the Course |
| Hole | 10 | 11 | 12 | 13 | 14 | 15 | 16 | 17 | 18 | In | Total |
| Yardage | 521 | 447 | 435 | 194 | 552 | 379 | 201 | 380 | 434 | 3,543 | 7,190 |
| Par | 5 | 4 | 4 | 3 | 5 | 4 | 3 | 4 | 4 | 36 | 72 |

## America's Best: Rater's Notebook

### 1. Ease and intimacy of routing: 7

The site dictated the out-and-back routing, with the best natural "rooms" to be found in two areas: the shared fairway corridor around the wash on Nos. 2 and 8 (both par 5s) and the wide pocket containing Nos. 10-11-12. There's a bit of lateral squeeze on some play areas.

### 2. Quality of feature shaping: 6

It's very hard to make shapes and contours appear subtle when they are hewn out of rocky areas and then set against such a dramatic background as this kind of desert hill country. Uphill areas are very well crafted and receptive to shots, though three holes (8, 14, 17) rely upon the identical triple bunker sequence on the right side to define an ascending playing area.

### 3. Natural setting and overall land plan: 8

Dramatic setting that does not overwhelm, so that you always can play golf while admiring the distant landforms. Clubhouse and practice range are situated at convergence point of nines and fit in unobtrusively.

### 4. Interest of greens and surrounding contours: 6

Modestly sized putting surfaces are well integrated into base contours, with most greens pitched slightly toward approach zones. Fleshy mounding behind greens and bunkers is a bit pronounced, however, and doesn't quite tie in to grades of native desert.

### 5. Variety and memorability of par 3s: 5

Three of the par 3s are used to bridge tough downhill terrain. The dramatic images of the sixth (right to left) and 16th (left to right) are fine, but the ninth looks too much like a resort poster and is at odds with the character of the rest of the course.

### 6. Variety and memorability of par 4s: 6

Fine mix of doglegs. Short par 4s on each side are used to ascend to high points. With the par 3s accounting for the bulk of the downhill slopes, only one full shot of the 20 on the par 4s (the tee shot at the 15th) plays downhill. Very good driving options, with placement sometimes more crucial than distance, as at Cape-hole No. 3.

### 7. Variety and memorability of par 5s: 6

Good diversity, especially on tee shot. Intervening wash on the eighth makes for an awkward (but unavoidable) separation of first and second fairways. The 521-yard 10th has a phenomenal shelf short of the green for smart layups. Best of all is the "over hill and dale" second shot on the 552-yard 14th.

### 8. Basic quality of conditioning: 8

Oddly for such a site, there was plenty of topsoil on hand, and it shows. A strong grow-in was followed by a successful overseed that doesn't allow the course to play slow and heavy in the winter.

### 9. Landscape and tree management: 9

Palo Verde trees dominate over cacti, giving it a slightly lusher feel than one finds on the arid desert floor.

### 10. "Walk in the park" test: 8

The first time around the course I played without yardage charts or distances and, simply eyeballing every shot, managed to get around fine. There's a generous feel to the course, enhanced by the sense that this is very much an outpost of the game in its early stages of establishment.

**Overall vote by *Golfweek* course raters: 6.91**

**Architect:** Rees Jones, 1991     **Superintendent:** Bob Ranum

# Atlantic Golf Club

## Bridgehampton, New York

| Par | 72 |
|---|---|
| Yards | 6,940 |
| Slope | 140 |
| Rating | 74.6 |

**Golfweek Rating**

**6.89**

The making of Atlantic Golf Club on the far eastern end of Long island's South Fork is as much a business epic as a golf story. In a recent book, *The Miracle on Breeze Hill*, club founder Lowell Schulman amply documents the paper trail involved in financing the $20 million project and negotiating the many hurdles of environmental permitting needed to complete the project.

The result is a linksy par-72 layout, 6,940 yards from the tips, that ambles across a 200-acre windswept site. Dense fescues frame every hole and highlight the strategic options of the bentgrass tees, fairways and greens.

The reverse Redan-style, 218-yard, par-3 fourth hole plays around the rim of a massive kettle hole. On the far northern corner of the converted farm that became Atlantic GC, wind plays havoc at the 127-yard, par-3 11th hole to the smallest green on the course. Befitting the setting, in the golf-rich Hamptons, the 609-yard, par-5 18th hole delivers golfers to a cozy East End-style shingle clubhouse. Atlantic's first foray in the national spotlight came in 1997 when it hosted the USGA Senior Amateur, won by Cliff Cunningham.

*—Bradley S. Klein*

# Cassique

## Kiawah Island, South Carolina

Most visitors to Cassique are shocked by the initial image of sharp, almost pyramidal mounding. And yet a few holes into a round at this distinctive course south of Charleston along the Intracoastal marshes and you realize that the angular features work as an essential part of the strategy.

Credit Tom Watson for not holding back on his first U.S. design effort. The result is a distinctive solution to a topographic problem, namely how to make the flat tomato field containing the front nine into interesting golf ground. The trick in construction was not simply to pop up the mounds for visual effect but to make their slopes integral to the playing character of the course. This is where Cassique excels. The 40-foot-high dunes framing holes three, four and five create the feel and sensibility of a wild Irish links course.

For all the boldness of these mounds, a certain restraint prevails. The deeper into the round you go, the softer the mounds become and the more the native marshland assume centrality. The bulk of the back nine assume a classical lowlands look, with the culmination coming at the 540-yard, par-5 15th hole, where mid-fairway bunkers on the first and second shot-landing areas define multiple options along a bulkheaded wetlands.

During construction, 65 mature live oaks were transplanted on site, endowing Cassique with an established look. The sensibility is enhanced by a clubhouse that looks like a 19th century English country manor.

*—Bradley S. Klein*

| Par | 72 |
|---|---|
| Yards | 6,996 |
| Slope | 137 |
| Rating | 74.2 |

*Golfweek* Rating
6.86

**Cassique**
*Kiawah Island, South Carolina*

# Contributors

**James Achenbach** of Portland, Oregon, is a boring, predictable guy who never wanted to be anything but a golf writer and got his wish. His friends continually remind him that golf is not played after dark. They tell him to get a life. After studying writing at the University of Iowa Writers Workshop, Achenbach moved to Florida to play golf and write about the game. He captured the championship of the Golf Writers Association of America and also won GWAA first-place writing awards in four different categories. He doesn't expect to get a life any time soon.

**Jeff Babineau** of Oviedo, Florida, is deputy editor at *Golfweek*, where he oversees the magazine's coverage of professional and amateur golf. Prior to joining *Golfweek* in 1998, Babineau worked at *The Orlando Sentinel* for 13 years, his last three spent covering golf, and in 1996 he heavily chronicled the Orlando arrival of a PGA Tour rookie by the name of Tiger Woods. Babineau also has covered the NFL's Tampa Bay Buccaneers and NHL's Tampa Bay Lightning, has written two children's books on hockey and in his spare time plays to a 6-index.

**Jeff Barr** is assistant managing editor at *Golfweek*, in charge of the magazine's feature section. Departments in the section include game improvement, equipment, architecture, course rating, life in private clubs and golf destinations. Barr spends most of his time in *Golfweek*'s Orlando office, but there is the occasional foray into the world of golf travel—all in the interest of serving *Golfweek* readers, of course. Barr has written a book, *Business Traveler's Guide to Golf* (1999), that details courses that are close to downtown areas or airports in 40 cities throughout the United States.

**Lynn Henning** insists he doesn't take his golf clubs to spring training when he covers the Detroit Tigers. An occasional contributor to *Golfweek* and "*Golfweek*'s SuperNews," he spends most of the time as a sports writer for the *Detroit News*, where his beats include all four major sports and university athletics. Henning is co-author (with Kirk Gibson) of *Bottom of the Ninth* and is solo author of *Spartan Seasons: Triumphs and Turmoils of Michigan State University Sports*.

**Scott Kauffman** has been a senior writer for *Golfweek* and "*Golfweek*'s SuperNews" since 1999. He specializes in golf course development, management and maintenance. Previously, Kauffman spent 12 years as a journalist with several newspapers, radio and television stations, including *USA Today* and *USA Today Baseball Weekly* (now *Sports Weekly*).

**Bradley S. Klein** of Bloomfield, Connecticut, is a former PGA Tour caddie and professor of political science who would rather be looking at golf courses. He has been architecture editor of *Golfweek* since 1988, runs that magazine's "America's Best" course rating program, and is also the founding editor of "*Golfweek*'s SuperNews." A frequent speaker at golf industry and club meetings, Klein has authored two golf books. *Rough Meditations* (1997) is a collection of his essays on caddying, travel and course design. *Discovering Donald Ross: the Architect and his Golf Courses* (2001) won the annual USGA International Book Award.

**Jeff Rude** is a *Golfweek* senior writer who specializes in covering the PGA Tour. In other words, he follows Tiger Woods around the world. He has covered the Tour in four different decades, though he's really not that old. Rude grew up in the Chicago area, attended the University of Missouri School of Journalism on an Evans Scholarship and caddied on the Tour in 1974. He currently carries an 8-index and resides in Flossmoor, Illinois, with a driver and a 3-wood from Olympia Fields, site of the 2003 U.S. Open.

**Dave Seanor** has been editor of *Golfweek* since 1994. A lifelong public golfer and more recently a collector of rare golf books, Seanor lives in Orlando, Florida, and plays to a 10-index. He is a former managing editor of *PGA Magazine* and spent 17 years in daily newspaper sports journalism, including stints with the *Chicago Sun-Times*, *New York Post* and *Detroit News*. His favorite course is New Castle Country Club (A. W. Tillinghast, 1923) in his hometown of New Castle, Pennsylvania.

**John Steinbreder** of Easton, Connecticut, is a senior writer at *Golfweek* and the author of six books. A 5-index who loves the great classic courses of Raynor, Macdonald, Tillinghast and MacKenzie, he usually reports on the business of golf. But he also composes a fair number of travel and feature articles for *Golfweek*, including a monthly column called "Club Life." He has been honored four times for his work by the Golf Writers Association of America.

# Photo Credits